AQA GCSE History

MEDIEVAL ENGLAND

The reign of Edward I 1272–1307

Alf Wilkinson

Approval message from AQA

This textbook has been approved by AQA for use with our qualification. This means that we have checked that it broadly covers the specification and we are satisfied with the overall quality. Full details of our approval process can be found on our website.

We approve textbooks because we know how important it is for teachers and students to have the right resources to support their teaching and learning. However, the publisher is ultimately responsible for the editorial control and quality of this book.

Please note that when teaching the *AQA GCSE History* course, you must refer to AQA's specification as your definitive source of information. While this book has been written to match the specification, it cannot provide complete coverage of every aspect of the course.

A wide range of other useful resources can be found on the relevant subject pages of our website: www.aqa.org.uk.

AN HACHETTE UK COMPANY

The Publishers would like to thank the following for permission to reproduce copyright material.

Photo credits

p.2 The Battle of Stirling, Jackson, Peter (1922-2003) / Private Collection / © Look and Learn / Bridgeman Images; **p.4** ©The Print Collector / HIP /TopFoto; **p.5** © British Library Board / TopFoto; **p.7** © The National Archives; **p.9** Courtesy of John D. Clare; **p. 10** © British Library Board / TopFoto; **p.12** © The British Library Board (Thompson MS 13, f. 74r); **p.14** © The British Library Board (Royal 20 C. VII, f.51); **p.15** *t* © Petar Milošević/Wikimedia Commons (supplied under Creative Commons license) *b* Crown copyright, National Records of Scotland, SP13/7; **p.16** ©The National Archives; **p.17** © British Library Board / TopFoto; **p.19** *t* © Heritage Image Partnership Ltd / Alamy Stock Photo *b* © Historic England Archive; **p.20** © The Granger Collection / TopFoto; **p.24** © British Library Board / TopFoto; **p.25** ©2005 Woodmansterne/TopFoto; **p.26** © British Library/The Art Archive; **p.27** © British Library Board (Royal 2. B.VII folio 74); **p.28** © Frank Naylor / Alamy Stock Photo; **p. 29** *t* © British Library Board / TopFoto *bl* Medieval fair (colour litho), Escott, Dan (1928-87) / Private Collection / © Look and Learn / Bridgeman Images *br* © British Library Board (Royal 10 E IV f. 58); **p.30** *t* ©TopFoto *m* © gameover / Alamy Stock Photo *b* © PHGCOM/Wikimedia COmmons (supplied under Creative Commons license); **p.31**© Master and Fellows of Corpus Christi College, Cambridge.; **p.32** © Historic England Archive; **p.33** *t* © Holmes Garden Photos / Alamy Stock Photo *b* © Andrew Barker / Alamy Stock Photo; **p.34** © The National Archives; **p.36** *t* © INTERFOTO / Alamy Stock Photo *m* ©TopFoto *b* © ianwool/123RF. com; **p.37** © Keith Heron / Alamy Stock Photo; **p.38** *tl* ©The British Library Board (Add. 42130 f.32) *tr* © Heritage Image Partnership Ltd. / Alamy Stock Photo *b* © Ann Ronan Pictures/Print Collector/ Getty Images; **p.39** © British Library / Science Photo Library; **p.40** © The Art Archive / Alamy Stock Photo; **p.41** © National Archives; **p.42** © Historic England Archive; **p.47** Courtesy of John D. Clare; **p.48** © Slow Images/Getty Images; **p.49** © schistra/Shutterstock; **p.50** © British Library Board / TopFoto; **p.51** © Hulton Archive/Getty Images; **p.52** *t* Reconstructional drawing from various sources by George Kruger Gray, via fromoldbooks.org *b* © A.P.S. (UK) / Alamy Stock Photo; **p.53** © Fine Art Images / Heritage Images / TopFoto; **p.56** © British Library Board / TopFoto; **p.58** *t* © Jeanette Teare/123RF. com *b* © Crown copyright (2016) Cadw; **p.59** Supplied by Llyfrgell Genedlaethol Cymru / National Library of Wales; **p.60** © Tony Trasmundi / Alamy Stock Photo; **p.62** f.6 John de Baliol and his wife from the Seton Armorial, 1591 (manuscript), English School, (16th century) /© National Library of Scotland, Edinburgh, Scotland / Bridgeman Images; **p.63** Portrait of William Wallace, c.1700 (oil on canvas), Scottish School, (18th century) / Private Collection / Photo © Christie's Images / Bridgeman Images; **p.64** ©TopFoto; **p.65** *t* © BusterBrownBB/Wikimedia (supplied under Creative Commons CC BY_SA 3.0 license). *b* ©2006 Matt Miller/TopFoto; **p.67** The Battle of Stirling, Jackson, Peter (1922-2003) / Private Collection / © Look and Learn / Bridgeman Images; **p.69** © Hulton Archive/Getty Images; **p.70** *t* © Justin Kase z04z / Alamy Stock Photo; *b* © miscellany / Alamy Stock Photo

ANote: The wording and sentence structure of some written sources have been adapted and simplified to make them accessible to all pupils while faithfully preserving the sense of the original.

Every effort has been made to trace all copyright holders, but if any have been inadvertently overlooked, the Publishers will be pleased to make the necessary arrangements at the first opportunity.

Although every effort has been made to ensure that website addresses are correct at time of going to press, Hodder Education cannot be held responsible for the content of any website mentioned in this book. It is sometimes possible to find a relocated web page by typing in the address of the home page for a website in the URL window of your browser.

Hachette UK's policy is to use papers that are natural, renewable and recyclable products and made from wood grown in sustainable forests. The logging and manufacturing processes are expected to conform to the environmental regulations of the country of origin.

Orders: please contact Bookpoint Ltd, 130 Milton Park, Abingdon, Oxon OX14 4SE. Telephone: +44 (0)1235 827720. Fax: +44 (0)1235 400454. Email education@bookpoint.co.uk Lines are open from 9 a.m. to 5 p.m., Monday to Saturday, with a 24-hour message answering service. You can also order through our website: www. hoddereducation.co.uk

ISBN: 978 1 4718 64261

© Alf Wilkinson 2016
First published in 2016 by
Hodder Education,
An Hachette UK Company
Carmelite House
50 Victoria Embankment
London EC4Y 0DZ

www.hoddereducation.co.uk

Impression number 10 9 8 7 6 5 4 3 2 1

Year   2020 2019 2018 2017 2016

Cover photo © Corbis/Lebrecht Music & Arts

Illustrations by DC Graphic Design Limited

Typeset in ITC Giovanni Std 9.5/12pt by DC Graphic Design Limited, Hextable, Kent

Printed in Italy

A catalogue record for this title is available from the British Library.

CONTENTS

HOW THIS BOOK WILL HELP YOU IN AQA GCSE HISTORY

It will help you to learn the content

The **author text** explains all the key content clearly and comprehensively. It helps you understand each period and each topic, and the themes that connect the topics.

The **Factfiles** and **Profiles** are packed with facts and examples to use in your own work to support your arguments.

We use lots of **diagrams** and **maps** to help you to visualise, understand and remember topics. We also encourage you to draw your own diagrams – that is an even better way to learn.

This book is full of brilliant **sources**. This course deals with some big issues but sources can help pin those issues down. History is at its best when you can see what real people said, did, wrote, sang, watched, laughed about, cried over and got upset about. Sources can really help you to understand the story better and remember it, because they help you to see the events and ideas in terms of what they meant to people at the time.

FIGURE 8

A modern illustration of the Battle of Stirling Bridge. It was drawn in 1976 for a children's story book.

SOURCE 5

English Exchequer Pipe Rolls, 1304–05; English Exchequer accounts, translated by Dr J.R. Davies.

John of Lincoln and Roger of Paris render account for the citizens of London …

THINK

1 How important were the infantry?
2 Which part of it was most important?
3 Why?

Throughout the book there are tasks which are designed to build your understanding of a period or issue step by step. **Think** questions direct you to the things you should be noticing or thinking about. They also practise the kind of analytical skills that you need to improve in history. They will help prepare you for the **Focus Tasks** – see opposite.

Key Words. Every subject and topic has its own vocabulary. If you don't know what these words mean you won't be able to write about the subject. So, for each topic we have provided a keywords list. You should aim to be able to understand them and use them confidently in your writing. They are all defined in the **Glossary** on pages 76–7. But we also want you to create your own keywords list – in a notebook or on your phone, write down each word with your *own* definition.

> **KEY WORDS**
>
> Make sure you know what these terms mean:
> - Feudal system
> - Model parliament
> - Rights
> - Justice

Finally there are **Tips** throughout to help you focus on the important issues and there is a **Topic Summary** at the end of every topic. This condenses all the content into a few points, which should help you to get your bearings in even the most complicated content. Some people say it is good to read the summary before you even start the topic so you know where you are heading.

> **TOPIC SUMMARY**
>
> **Trade, towns and villages**
> - England was fast becoming a cash economy at this time, after 30 years of good harvests.
> - Towns and trade were increasingly important.

It will help you to apply what you learn

The second big aim of this book is to help you apply what you learn, which means to help you think deeply about the content and develop your own judgements about the issues, and make sure you can support those judgements with evidence and relevant knowledge.

This is not an easy task. You will not suddenly develop this skill. You need to practise studying an issue, deciding what you think, and then selecting from all that you know the points that are really relevant to your argument. One of the most important skills in history is the ability to select, organise and deploy (use) knowledge to answer a particular question.

The main way we help you with this is through the **Focus Tasks**. These are the big tasks that appear at the beginning and end of most topics. They bring together your learning and help you turn it into something memorable and creative. Part 1 (at the start of each topic) helps you make notes and gather information as you read; Part 2 (at the end of each topic) gets you to use your notes to analyse what you have learned and complete some written work. Both stages are important – gathering and organising the information and using it to show your understanding of it.

Most Focus Tasks have tips that help you get started – highlighting a couple of key points that you can use in your answers.

> **FOCUS TASK**
>
> **Why was Edward able to defeat the Welsh? Part 1**
>
> As you work through this topic:
>
> 1 Make a list of factors that enabled the English to defeat the Welsh. For each factor you find, make a card with a title and brief bullet points on it.
> 2 For each factor, decide if it shows English strength or Welsh weakness. Split the cards into two piles as you work through the topic.

It will help you review your learning and prepare for assessment

The **Chapter Review** at the end of each chapter introduces different styles of question used for assessment and provides practice questions to develop your skills.

Assessment Focus appears on pages 72–5. These pages take you step by step through the requirements of the specification and show you the kinds of questions you might be asked. We have also analysed some sample answers.

William Camden 1551–1623

- William Camden was born in London and studied at Oxford University.
- He was an antiquarian (dealer in antiques and rare books) and historian, who published *Britannia* in 1586.
- This was an attempt to describe Britain, county by county, both as it was then, and how it had been in history.
- The book was so successful it ran into many editions, and Camden spent his life updating it and writing more books.
- His fieldwork and research were novel at the time, but much copied since.
- His works continued to be published right into the nineteenth century.

THINK

1 What does this story tell us about Edward?
2 What does it tell us about Edward's relationship with Eleanor?
3 What does it tell us about the reliability of historians' writings?
4 What does it tell us about interpretations in history?

Introduction

In 1268, Edward 'took the cross' and promised to go to the HOLY LAND and fight the Muslims who were in control of much of the area. It took a long time to raise the money needed but eventually, in 1270, he and his wife Eleanor of Castile, along with around 1,000 men, arrived in Acre, one of the last remaining strongholds of the Christian community in the area.

After a few minor skirmishes, Edward realised that his forces were not big enough to defeat the Muslims so began negotiating a truce. While these negotiations were going on, messengers went back and forth between the two camps and the truce was finally signed in May 1272.

Edward decided to stay in Acre for a while to see if the truce held. One evening he was alone in his tent when a Muslim messenger arrived. The messenger tried to kill Edward with a poisoned dagger, but Edward managed to overpower him and kill him. Grievously ill, Edward began to put his affairs in order, expecting the worst. The only cure was to remove the poison from the wound in Edward's arm.

The story goes that Eleanor personally sucked the poison out from the wound to ensure Edward's safety. The nineteenth-century illustration below pictures the scene. Unfortunately, this story is almost certainly untrue! The wound was most likely cleaned out by one of Edward's doctors. The first recorded telling of this 'sucking out the poison' story is by William Camden (see Profile) in the late seventeenth century. It was then repeated by many writers until more recent research has shown the story to be completely without foundation.

Whatever actually happened, we do know is that after several weeks' CONVALESCENCE, in September 1272, Edward and Eleanor set off for England. On the way they discovered that Edward's father Henry III had died in November 1272 and that Edward was now King of England.

FIGURE 1

A map of the Ninth Crusade.

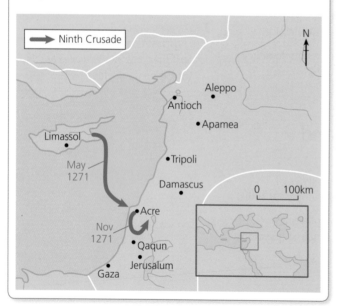

SOURCE 2

A nineteenth-century illustration of Eleanor sucking the poison from Edward's arm, thus saving his life.

This British Depth Study gives you the opportunity to explore the life and reign of one of the most remarkable Plantagenet kings of England – Edward 'Longshanks' or Edward I.

Born in 1239, he became king in 1272 and ruled until his death in 1307. Unusually for someone of Norman descent, he was named Edward after Edward the Confessor, the last Saxon king of England, who his father greatly admired. When he was only fifteen his father arranged for him to marry Eleanor of Castile.

His father, Henry III, was a weak king, and his reign saw constant conflict between king and barons. In 1264, Henry was deposed for a short while and kept prisoner by Simon de Montfort until 1265. Then in 1265 de Montfort was defeated at the Battle of Evesham by an army led by Prince Edward. Simon was brutally killed and Henry III restored to the throne.

That battle established Edward's reputation as a great fighter and much of his reign was taken up with war.

As king he conquered Wales, making it effectively part of England. He failed in his attempts to do the same with Scotland but never gave up. He even died, in Burgh-on-the-Sands, near Carlisle on 7 July 1307, on the way to invade Scotland again! Edward was also ruler of Gascony, now part of France, and had continual disputes with the King of France.

War was expensive so Edward was always short of money and towards the end of his reign, the cost of his wars led to many disputes with his subjects.

Nevertheless, in the early part of his reign, Edward was viewed as a shrewd politician, someone who listened to complaints and acted on injustices. At one stage, he even removed every one of the sheriffs before introducing an enquiry into CORRUPTION. He tried hard to make the law accessible to all, rich or poor, even if his main aim was to maintain the power and authority of the king.

SOURCE 3

Edward and his wife, Eleanor, from an early fourteenth-century manuscript. This is one of few contemporary images of Edward.

PROFILE

Eleanor of Castile, 1241–90

- Eleanor was born in Spain, the second daughter of King Ferdinand III.
- She was brought up at court and educated, which was unusual at the time.
- In 1254 she was married to the future Edward I.
- Despite having an ARRANGED MARRIAGE, they seemed to be very much in love and had sixteen children, although many did not survive childhood.
- She accompanied Edward on his Crusade, where one of their children, Joan of Acre, was born.
- She was not popular in England, largely because of the way she acquired so much land, but Edward was devastated when she died in 1290.

FOCUS TASK

What kind of king will Edward be?

This is what people expected of a medieval king:

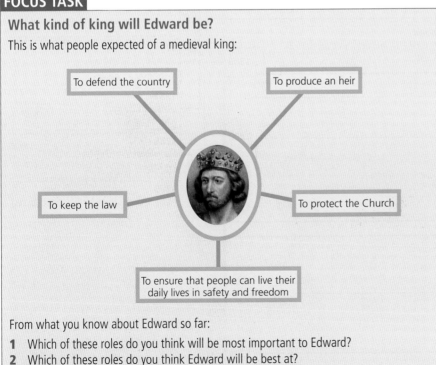

To defend the country

To produce an heir

To keep the law

To protect the Church

To ensure that people can live their daily lives in safety and freedom

From what you know about Edward so far:

1. Which of these roles do you think will be most important to Edward?
2. Which of these roles do you think Edward will be best at?
3. What do you expect to be the major issues explored in this depth study?
4. Finally, at this point, what kind of king do you think Edward will be?

Edward's life

This timeline shows some of the main events you will be studying in this book and how the different strands relate to each other.

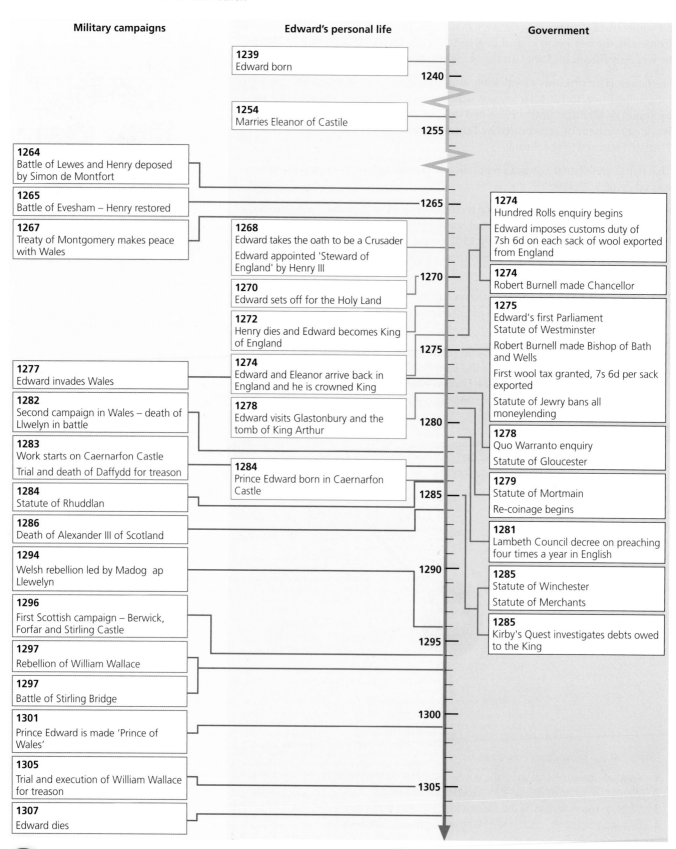

Military campaigns

1264
Battle of Lewes and Henry deposed by Simon de Montfort

1265
Battle of Evesham – Henry restored

1267
Treaty of Montgomery makes peace with Wales

1277
Edward invades Wales

1282
Second campaign in Wales – death of Llwelyn in battle

1283
Work starts on Caernarfon Castle
Trial and death of Daffydd for treason

1284
Statute of Rhuddlan

1286
Death of Alexander III of Scotland

1294
Welsh rebellion led by Madog ap Llewelyn

1296
First Scottish campaign – Berwick, Forfar and Stirling Castle

1297
Rebellion of William Wallace

1297
Battle of Stirling Bridge

1301
Prince Edward is made 'Prince of Wales'

1305
Trial and execution of William Wallace for treason

1307
Edward dies

Edward's personal life

1239
Edward born

1254
Marries Eleanor of Castile

1268
Edward takes the oath to be a Crusader
Edward appointed 'Steward of England' by Henry III

1270
Edward sets off for the Holy Land

1272
Henry dies and Edward becomes King of England

1274
Edward and Eleanor arrive back in England and he is crowned King

1278
Edward visits Glastonbury and the tomb of King Arthur

1284
Prince Edward born in Caernarfon Castle

Government

1274
Hundred Rolls enquiry begins
Edward imposes customs duty of 7sh 6d on each sack of wool exported from England

1274
Robert Burnell made Chancellor

1275
Edward's first Parliament
Statute of Westminster
Robert Burnell made Bishop of Bath and Wells
First wool tax granted, 7s 6d per sack exported
Statute of Jewry bans all moneylending

1278
Quo Warranto enquiry
Statute of Gloucester

1279
Statute of Mortmain
Re-coinage begins

1281
Lambeth Council decree on preaching four times a year in English

1285
Statute of Winchester
Statute of Merchants

1285
Kirby's Quest investigates debts owed to the King

Timeline dates (right axis): 1240, 1255, 1265, 1270, 1275, 1280, 1285, 1290, 1295, 1300, 1305

Government: The rights of king and people

1

Edward was only 33 when he became king, inheriting a country whose stability had been shakily restored after a civil war between king and barons. But by 1295, Edward had assembled a 'Model Parliament' and was doing his best to provide justice in England.

This chapter will examine the legacy Edward inherited and his efforts to restore the king's authority and provide rights and justice for the people.

England in 1272

The power of the king

The Normans introduced the FEUDAL SYSTEM to England (see Figure 1). The king owned all the land and that was the source of his wealth and power. He granted land to his followers, in exchange for OBLIGATIONS: to swear loyalty to the king; to fight for the king when required; to pay taxes; and to keep the countryside safe. Most followers received several pieces of land, spread across the country so they would not become too powerful in one area and strong enough to challenge the king. The exception to this was in the border regions – the Welsh Marches and northern England – where strong local landowners were needed to stop invasions (see Figure 2). These Marcher Lords, as they became known, were a powerful and sometimes disruptive influence on society, often trying to extend their power and wealth at the expense of their neighbours. Lots of land was also set aside as Royal Forests, for example, the New Forest in Hampshire, kept for the king to go hunting.

In turn, the king's chief supporters (the barons) would grant land, usually a local manor, to each of their knights, in exchange for support. The knights would have to fight for the baron, protect his CASTLES and so on. The knight's wealth came from the peasants, or VILLEINs, who did the actual farming and who would have to work for the knight, without pay, for three or four days every week in exchange for the land they farmed but did not own. That way the king kept personal control of everything!

Things were beginning to change, however. Sheep were becoming more profitable so landowners wanted grazing not farming land, and were sometimes more likely to rent land to villeins who might then be able to become freemen.

The Church

Over time, the Church became a great landowner as the king and the barons granted land and money to build churches and monasteries. There were even Church courts to try priests who broke the law. Monasteries were, in effect, the hospitals of the time, as monks developed expertise in dealing with disease. Many of the king's advisers and officials were clerics, because they were the ones who could read *and* write. In medieval England, the Church, and thus the Pope, was a powerful and wealthy influence.

Agriculture

In 1272 the population of England was around 4.75 million, probably the biggest it had ever been. Most people lived in the countryside and worked in agriculture. Much of the country's wealth was dependent upon sheep. The wool TRADE made many merchants rich. They traded with the LOW COUNTRIES (see Figure 2) especially, and much of Europe. Land was being turned over to grazing, which was more profitable than growing crops.

FIGURE 1

The feudal system.

```
                    KING
  Provide                      Grants
  money                        lands to
  and
  knights
                   BARONS
  Provide                      Grant
  protection                   land to
  and
  military
  service
                   KNIGHTS
  Provide                      Grant the
  food and                     use of
  services                     land to

                  PEASANTS
```

FIGURE 2

England, the Welsh Marches and the Low Countries in the 1200s.

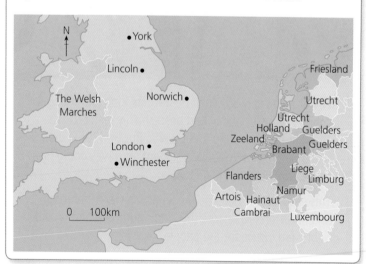

York

Lincoln

Friesland

The Welsh Marches

Norwich

Utrecht

Utrecht
Holland   Guelders
Zeeland   Guelders
         Brabant

London

Winchester

Liege
Limburg

Flanders

Namur

Artois   Hainaut

Cambrai   Luxembourg

N

0   100km

Towns

Towns were growing. London had a population of perhaps 10,000 at this time, followed by Winchester (6,000), York, Lincoln and Norwich (each 5,000), although still very small by modern standards. Many villeins tried to escape to the towns because if you could survive for a year without being sent back to your village, you were usually free to stay. Life was freer in the towns, but illness was more of a risk. Tuberculosis and other infectious diseases spread quickly in the unsanitary urban conditions.

Craftsmen and merchants tended to live in the towns and ports, and workers of the same trade would live and work together in one street or part of the town, like the Shambles in York, which was where the butchers congregated. GUILDS of craftsmen became quite powerful, restricting the numbers of APPRENTICES, for example, to keep wages high.

Diet

Most people lived on or near the poverty line, eating bread and pottage, a kind of stew made from beans, peas and oats, with herbs or a little meat or fish if available. Rabbit, chicken and fish were sometimes eaten, but the penalties for poaching were severe. A bad harvest meant difficult times for many people. Better-off people would eat meat as much as they could (often suffering constipation as a result!) and refused to eat vegetables which were thought to be poor people's food. Pigeons were kept in big dovecotes, and fish in 'stews' or fishponds. Rabbits were kept in huge warrens. Many animals would be slaughtered in the autumn because of a lack of winter fodder.

THINK

Study Figure 3.

1 Can you spot all the hazards facing those living in a medieval town?
2 How accurate do you think this interpretation of town life is?
3 England was a wealthy country in 1272, but not as wealthy as other European countries like Italy. What was the source of England's wealth?
4 How equally was this wealth shared out? Which groups were doing well and which were struggling?
5 In what ways is the impression of England you get from these pages similar to, and different from, what you already know about medieval England?

FIGURE 3

A modern interpretation of a medieval town.

1.1 Henry III's legacy

FOCUS

Edward was born into a divided family and a divided kingdom. His father, Henry III, had taken the country to civil war over disagreements with the barons. Henry had even been deposed for a few months. In this topic you will explore:

● how Henry had tried to re-establish royal authority and how far he had succeeded.
● how well prepared Edward was for the challenges of ruling England.

Henry III's efforts to restore royal authority

Source 1 is from a famous medieval manuscript. It is a picture of ANARCHY. At the top barons are fighting barons, at the bottom peasants are fighting peasants. This was how things were in Henry III's reign. It was going to be a tough task to restore control. This is how Henry tried to do it. You judge how far he succeeded.

The barons

Simon de Montfort and an army of barons had defeated Henry at the Battle of Lewes in 1264. Simon was in turn defeated by Prince Edward at Evesham in 1265, thus putting Henry III back on the throne.

At first rebel barons were treated very harshly. Henry gave the lands of 316 rebels to 133 individuals who had supported him. The rebels were told they would never recover their lands. This was a good way to please his supporters but a bad way to win back the rebels' loyalty. It merely prolonged the rebellion.

Prince Edward realised this and pushed for a more merciful approach. Some rebels were forgiven if they laid down their arms rather than fight. Most were allowed to buy back their lands under a process known as REDEMPTION. Depending how guilty they were judged to be by the King, redemption might cost anything between two and seven years' income. This was a hefty sum, but at least there was the chance to 'buy back' your lands and thus be reintegrated into society. Money to pay redemption payments could be borrowed either from the king himself or from Jewish money-lenders.

Being hugely in debt to the king was another way Henry could ensure support from the barons. If they didn't behave well enough, they could be asked to pay back their debt all in one go, something most were unable to do.

SOURCE 1

Illustration from the *Holkham Bible Picture Book*, circa 1320.

FOCUS TASK

How well prepared was Edward to be king? Part 1

As you work through pages 10–13, make notes in your own copy of the following table, on whether or not Edward was well prepared to be king.

Well prepared	Not well prepared

Crusade

Henry III had promised to go on a crusade in the 1250s but never did, as he was either short of funds or not in a strong enough position to leave the country for any length of time. Now he saw a Crusade as one way to restore unity to the country. It was hoped that if former rebels and supporters of the King would join Prince Edward on Crusade they would forget their differences. This plan did not really work. Edward went on Crusade in 1270 and a few rebels did go but most could not afford to leave the country for any length of time as they were trying to keep up their redemption payments in order to regain their lands. However the fact that Edward was able to go on Crusade at all shows how conditions in the country had changed for the better by 1270.

Parliament and taxes

Another measure of Henry's degree of control is the attitude of the clergy and Parliament to requests for taxation to pay for this Crusade.

- In 1267 the clergy voted one-twentieth of their income as a tax to the King, to finance Prince Edward's Crusade.
- In 1270 the LAY MEMBERS of Parliament also voted one-twentieth as a tax to pay for the Crusade.

These votes gave the king some financial stability and reflect the more settled conditions. However they were only granted because Henry agreed to act on some of the GRIEVANCES brought before him in Parliament. There still wasn't enough money to fund the Crusade so Edward had to borrow from King Philip of France (funded from the customs duties of trade in Gascony) and the Pope.

Wales

There was peace between England and Wales after a long period of conflict. In the Treaty of Montgomery of 1267, Henry recognised the right of Llywelyn ap Gruffudd to be known as the Prince of Wales, providing Llywelyn did HOMAGE to Henry III (which meant acknowledging him as his feudal overlord). This brought to an end the long-running dispute between England and Wales over borders and the right to rule. However, the Treaty didn't stop the Marcher Lords from continuing their sniping for advantage in the area.

Succession

A final indication of how far royal authority had been restored was that when Henry III died in 1272, Edward's succession was assured. No one opposed him, and although Edward was away on Crusade he felt no need to rush home and be crowned as other heirs to the throne before him had done. In fact he took nearly two years to come home, following a leisurely journey across Europe including a stay in Gascony to settle his affairs there.

THINK

1 In your opinion, was Henry III a strong king?
2 How successful was Henry in restoring his authority?

Was Edward ready to be king?

There are few surviving records of Edward's childhood or upbringing. However, we do know that:

- when he was eight he was given permission to hunt in Windsor Forest (probably using a falcon as in the scene in Source 2).
- he had a special suit of armour and weapons made for him to participate in a tournament in 1256.
- he could read – we have records of him borrowing chivalric romances from his mother – and speak French, Anglo-Norman, Latin and English.

He was married in 1254, given lands by his father for the occasion and knighted by his Spanish father-in-law. We also know that his father kept a tight rein on the lands he gave to Edward, who as a consequence was always short of money. Edward had a difficult relationship with his father, always wanting more money, authority or control over his own affairs and sometimes even aligning himself with opponents of Henry.

SOURCE 2

A lady hunting using a falcon, from an illuminated manuscript, in the early fourteenth century.

Edward's character

No-one seems to have had a good opinion of Edward as a young man. He is described as a 'swaggering youth', selfish, arrogant and only interested in himself. He spent much time and money with a RETINUE of like-minded knights, often 200-strong (see Source 3). He changed his mind readily when it suited him, although he did play a part in defeating a Welsh rebellion in 1256 (see Source 4).

THINK

Study Sources 3 and 4.

1. What do these two sources tell us about Edward?
2. How do they agree? How do they disagree?
3. How useful are these sources in telling us about Edward at that time?
4. Using these two sources, would you agree that Edward was not ready to be king in 1264?
5. To what extent does Source 5 agree with Matthew Paris (Source 3) and the author of the *Song of Lewes* (Source 4), and to what extent does it disagree?
6. How might you decide which source is more useful in our current enquiry?

SOURCE 3

Historia Anglorum, by Matthew Paris, written circa 1255. Paris was a monk at St Albans Abbey, where he wrote this and other works. He knew Henry III and other notables and obtained much of his information from them.

Edward's retainers and followers disturbed the peace of the inhabitants of the country through which they passed by plundering their possessions as well as abusing their persons ... For the ruffians and robbers whom he kept in his court spread themselves far and wide and forcibly seized and carried off the horses and carts of traders and the provisions of the inhabitants and out of the many acts of injustice perpetrated by his agents I have thought it worthwhile to mention the particulars of one to the readers. When the said Edward went to Earl Richard he found him at Wallingford where he was received with civility and entertained as a guest in the castle. His retainers in the meantime forced their way into the priory adjacent to the castle rudely and by force and not asking hospitality as was the custom then irreverently pushing the monks aside they seized on all that was necessary for supplying their table, fuel, and fodder for their horses, broke the doors, windows, and seats, insulted abused and beat the servants of the monks as though they had been slaves or convicted thieves and drove them from the place and scarcely allowed the monks themselves the use of the REFECTORY, the parlour being filled with those eating and the DORMITORY with those drinking.

A different side of Edward's character can be seen in instructions he sent to the Justiciar (administrator of Justice) of Chester in August 1259 (see Source 5).

SOURCE 4

An extract from *The Song of Lewes*, an English poem, written around 1264, by a supporter of Simon de Montfort after Simon defeated Henry and Edward at the Battle of Lewes.

Whereunto shall the noble Edward be compared? Perhaps he will be rightly called a leopard. If we divide the name it becomes lion and pard; lion, because we saw that he was not slow to attack the strongest places, fearing the onslaught of none, with the boldest valour making a raid amidst the castles, and wherever he goes succeeding as it were at his wish … A lion by pride and fierceness, he is by inconstancy and changeableness a pard, changing his word and promise, cloaking himself by pleasant speech. When he is in a strait he promises whatever you wish, but as soon as he has escaped he renounces his promise. The treachery or falsehood whereby he is advanced he calls prudence; the way whereby he arrives whither he will, crooked though it be, is regarded as straight; wrong gives him pleasure and is called right; whatever he likes he says is lawful, and he thinks that he is released from law, as though he were greater than the King…

SOURCE 5

Edward, writing to the Justiciar of Chester, August 1259.

… if common justice is denied to any of our subjects by us or by our bailiffs, we lose the favour both of God and man, and our lordship is belittled.

Edward's actions in the civil war

The Civil War of 1264–65 enhanced Edward's reputation as a soldier and leader. Historian Marc Morris suggests he emerged at the end of the war the most powerful figure in English politics and, at the Parliament of Winchester in 1268, Edward was made Steward of England by his father, surely in recognition of the part he played in running the country.

Edward's religious beliefs

Edward was also, as we might suspect from him undertaking a Crusade, deeply religious. On a particularly rough crossing of the Channel in the winter of 1263 or 1264, Edward promised if he survived he would found a religious house in thanks for God's deliverance. He duly endowed a Cistercian Abbey at Darnhall, in Cheshire. The site proved unsuitable for building and later the Abbey moved to Vale Royal. Edward and Eleanor laid some of the foundation stones of the Abbey.

FOCUS TASK

How well prepared was Edward to be king? Part 2

You have now completed your table on how well prepared Edward was to be king. Use it to answer these questions.

1. To what extent does R.F. Treherne's interpretation of Edward (Source 6) reflect the evidence on Edward in this topic?
2. Which sources does he seem to have used to construct his interpretation?
3. Which sources does he seem to have ignored?
4. Do you agree with Treherne or not?
5. Finally, use your findings from your table to answer the question: 'How well prepared was Edward to be king?'

SOURCE 6

R.F. Treherne, in his book *Baronial Plan of Reform*, published in 1972, describing Edward.

Edward was no more than an irresponsible, arrogant and headstrong boy, treacherously selfish in the heedless pursuit of his own ends, indulging in every whim at his own pleasure, and incapable of self-discipline or obedience to external authority in anything that conflicted with the passions and hatreds of the moment.

TOPIC SUMMARY

Henry III's legacy

- Henry's reign was one of conflict between the King and barons.
- Henry was deposed by Simon de Montfort and some of the barons in 1264.
- Edward grew up in a difficult environment but proved himself a great soldier and leader in the Civil War.
- Some people at the time were not favourably impressed by Edward's behaviour.

THINK

1 What do the events in Boston in 1288 tell us about the problems of LAW AND ORDER in medieval England?

2 Why would it have been difficult to identify and capture the offenders?

3 Opinion at the time differed as to whether the riot was a prank that got out of hand, with devastating consequences, or an audacious attempt to rob the merchants under the disguise of a tournament. What do you think?

4 Does this incident suggest there was 'good government' in England or not?

SOURCE 1

A criminal being hanged, from an illustration from a medieval manuscript.

FOCUS TASK A

Why is Edward called 'The English Justinian'?

Justinian was a famous Roman Emperor who reformed the legal system of ancient Rome (see Profile). Some historians have compared Edward I with Justinian. As you work through pages 15–17 gather evidence that shows why he might deserve this title.

1.2 The development of government, rights and justice

FOCUS

Some historians regard Edward as a king who completely altered both the way government was run, and the way the law operated. They call him 'the English Justinian', after the Roman emperor (see Profile). Others see him as a selfish king, solely interested in restoring those RIGHTS, lands and duties lost to the barons by his father Henry III. Still others see in him a PRAGMATIC desire to respond to injustices and make life fairer for everyone in England. This topic examines his actions and will help you decide which, if any, of these interpretations is right.

A riot at Boston Fair

In July 1288 Boston FAIR was in full swing. Throughout the month of July, Boston held what was probably the biggest fair in the country as over one-third of England's wool, especially that from Lincolnshire and the East of England, was exported from Boston, mostly to the Low Countries (see Source 2, page 8). Merchants came from across the known world to trade at the month-long fair. The fair was so successful that King's Lynn, in nearby Norfolk, complained that its fair was fading away!

On 26 July some local squires decided to organise a tournament. To make it more interesting they decided one side would dress up as monks from the local Greyfriars monastery, whilst the other side would dress up as CANONS from St Botolph's church. Being in disguise would make it more difficult to identify those taking part, and allow them to hide weapons under their monk's clothes. During the tournament one of them decided to help themselves to some of the goods on display at the fair, and others quickly followed. As the merchants attempted to gather up their goods, one merchant's tent caught fire. The fire rapidly spread and part of the town burned down. A riot ensued, as the people of Boston decided to help themselves to whatever they could, while they had the chance. There were several deaths. As one contemporary chronicle recorded, 'it was said that all the money in England could scarcely make good the damages, for rivers of gold and silver flowed into the sea'. The perpetrators fled by boat up the River Witham although one, Robert Chamberlain, was caught as he tried to make his escape. He refused to name any of the others involved in the riot, and was later tried and convicted of armed robbery, and hanged in public (like the criminal in Source 1).

Edward's promise

King Edward was crowned on 19 August 1274 in Westminster Abbey. The celebrations went on for a fortnight. It is said that after the Archbishop of Canterbury placed the crown of England on his head, Edward removed it stating that 'he would not wear it again until he had recovered the lands given away by his father to the earls, barons and knights of England, and to ALIENS'. According to the Dunstable Chronicler Edward had arrived in England 'full of reforming zeal'. The Bury St Edmunds Chronicler said he was 'energetic, generous and triumphant, like another Solomon' (a reference to King Solomon in the Bible). The historian Edmund King states that Edward 'came to insist that all within the British Isles acknowledge the superiority of his jurisdiction'. Expectations were high, especially after the splintering of authority under Henry III.

The 'Ragman Rolls'

Almost immediately after he returned to England, Edward decided to investigate abuses of power and encroachment of royal rights. Most of the sheriffs and escheators (officials responsible for wardships and estates that came to the Crown for administration and brought in a lot of money to the King) were replaced, and it was later found that many had abused their position. Some offences seemed quite trivial. The sheriff of Essex, for example, had seized eight cockerels because, he said, they might be used to fly into London and set fire to the city. Other abuses were much more serious. The sheriff of Yorkshire was accused of conspiring with the keeper of the prison in York to extract illegal payments from Wylkes de Gloseburne by tying him naked to a stake in York prison and starving him until he agreed to pay. Or the Prior (head of the priory) of Spalding who imprisoned Thomas de Algakirke until his feet rotted off. There were many more examples of such abuses, and the volume had increased during the new King's absence.

Investigating corruption

Removing corrupt officials was seen as a way of encouraging people to bring forward their complaints. Commissioners were then sent out all around the country, hundred by hundred (see Factfile below), to ask people a long list of around fifty questions, most of which were to do with royal landholdings. Edward wanted to know what land he owned, what rights he had, what customs were due to him, and especially, where rights had been alienated by others, usually as a result of weak government during his father's reign. He especially wanted to know about land ownership and feudal rights, as land was the basis of power and wealth. Land ownership often gave the power to hold courts, collect tolls, even carry out justice, all of which could be very lucrative. Land ownership might also confer the right *not* to do something. It might, for instance, give you the right not to attend the King's court, or not to provide him with knights or men at arms, so it was equally important to establish who had the right not to do things too! Edward also said that he intended to enforce good government.

Delivering complaints

Complaints and returns were delivered to London hundred by hundred, hence the name: the 'Hundred Rolls'. Some of these rolls still remain in the National Archives in Kew. They were also known as 'Ragman Rolls', because of all the seals of witnesses attached to them and dangling below the text (see Source 2). The exercise was repeated in 1279, in an echo of William the Conqueror's *Domesday Book* survey, but neither enquiry resulted in much change, as the Dunstable Chronicler stated, 'Nothing useful came of it'.

Hundreds

Each county was split into several smaller areas for administration. Each of these areas was called a 'hundred'. Dating from the tenth century, this area was the basis for law courts and keeping the peace, as well as government administration and tax raising.

THINK

5 Does the evidence suggest there was 'bad government' in England at this time?
6 In your opinion were the commissioners interested in rooting out corruption or were they looking out for Edward's rights?

PROFILE

Emperor Justinian, 482–565

- Justinian was emperor of what was left of the Roman Empire, based in Constantinople.
- He set out to restore the Roman Empire, and his generals conquered many countries.
- He also set out to reform Roman law, and his Code remains the basis of law in many countries today.

SOURCE 2

A 'Ragman Roll' showing all the seals attached to the document by those witnesses who had given evidence to the commissioners.

FOCUS TASK B

In what ways did Parliament change during Edward's reign? Part 1

1 As you work through pages 16–17 create your own spider diagram showing the changes in Parliament during the period 1272 to 1295.
2 Highlight these changes in three different colours:
 – changes that increased Edward's power
 – changes that increased the Lords' power
 – changes that increased the Commons' power.

SOURCE 3

An image of Edward I legislating, from a medieval manuscript from Malmesbury Abbey.

THINK

2 Which provisions of the Statute of Westminster suggest Edward is listening to the people?
3 Which provisions suggest he is interested in his own rights?
4 Do the provisions in the Statute of Westminster change your opinion of the main aims of Edward I once he became king?

Edward's first Parliament

Despite the Dunstable Chronicler's view that, 'Nothing useful came of it,' there were actions as a result of the Hundred Rolls survey. Edward summoned his first Parliament, in Westminster, in April 1275 so that he might 'set to rights the state of his kingdom', as he declared in the STATUTE of Westminster. It was perhaps the biggest parliament of the entire medieval period. It is estimated that 800 people were invited to attend, although we have no way of knowing exactly how many did turn up. No official records were kept until later. As well as the usual earls, barons and knights, bishops and abbots, Edward invited two BURGESSES (people living and having property rights in a town) from each town, and two knights from every shire. Some sources claim he invited four burgesses and four knights – he obviously wanted representatives from the whole country! There were two main reasons for inviting so many people: Edward wanted a TAX on merchants to help pay off his Crusading debts; and he wanted as many people as possible to be made aware of his first major piece of legislation, the Statute of Westminster.

The Statute of Westminster, 1275

The Statute of Westminster initially dealt with many of the abuses his Hundred Roll Commissioners had discovered. In total it had 51 chapters dealing with a huge variety of issues that had been brought to the King's attention since he arrived in England and deemed worthy of attention. Included in the Statute were provisions for dealing with unwanted guests in religious houses; tolls; abuse of WARDSHIP and PURVEYANCE (the right of the King to take goods when necessary to support himself or his army); the law regarding WRECKS; free elections; how sheriffs must act honestly, and a whole lot more.

What seems at first sight to be a mishmash of contradictory aims and ideas is, in reality, a response to many of the complaints to the King about corrupt officials, about abuses of the law, about unfair treatment before the law, and the treatment of criminals. Perhaps one of the key provisions was the introduction of the 'Hue and Cry', where every man in a neighbourhood must be prepared to pursue FELONS if the hue and cry is raised. A whole range of measures were targeted at sheriffs and other local officials in an attempt to ensure good government.

Convening the first Parliament of Edward's reign

The reason for inviting so many people to Parliament was to help publicise the provisions of the Statute of Westminster. All present were required to give their approval to its contents. The Statute was also to be read out in every local court, market places in towns and cities, and anywhere else local officials thought it ought to be read out. The message was clear: the King has listened to many of your complaints and now he is doing something about them. The Statute was the first of many, some like this one that covered a wide range of topics, and others very much single-issue statutes.

Edward pushes through more changes

Quo Warranto

Deeply in debt, Edward continued to send out officials to enquire about infringements of royal rights throughout the rest of his reign. The 'Quo Warranto' ('By what right?') enquiry of 1278 is typical. Landholders were asked to prove they had the right to land or dues they claimed. This was followed in 1285 by officials demanding to see the charter by which such land had been granted. The Earl of Gloucester is said to have brandished a rusty sword before officials, claiming it had come to England with his ancestors and William the Conqueror, and that his lands were given to him after the Conquest. That, he claimed, was all the title he needed! Many could not prove ownership and consequently, as a chronicler recorded, 'a great many men who did not have charters lost, without recovery, liberties and free customs of which they had been seized for a long time before'.

Statutes of Mortmain

In 1285 in an action known as 'Kirby's Quest' after the TREASURER of the time, officials tried to discover the extent of debts owed to the Crown, in an attempt to raise more money. In 1279 (and again in 1290, suggesting the action initially wasn't very successful) the Statutes of Mortmain tried to prevent land passing to the Church without the King's permission. The Church owned about 30 per cent of the land in England. Landowners were granting their land to the Church and receiving it back to use in their lifetime, or even in PERPETUITY. As the Church didn't pay a due to the King to inherit land when the owner died, or it changed hands, this meant Edward was losing out on taxes and feudal obligations. The Statute of Mortmain was an attempt to close this legal loophole, which landowners were using to deprive the King, as he saw it, of his feudal rights.

Statute of Westminster, 1285

There was another Statute of Westminster in 1285. The Statute of Westminster addressed grievances brought to the King's notice, including such weighty issues as fishing for salmon out of season. It aimed to make redress by the law speedier, and travel safer, for example, trees and woodland beside each road was to be cleared to prevent criminals hiding there and attacking travellers. One provision dealt with the crime of rape, and another of carrying away a nun from her abode. In all, there were 50 separate provisions. It clearly shows Edward listening to, and then responding to issues brought to his attention.

Statute of Merchants

The Statute of Merchants in 1285 built on the Statute of Acton Burnell in 1283 and was an attempt to deal with a very specific problem, namely the payment of debt between two merchants. The debtor was liable to have his goods seized or be imprisoned if he did not pay the debt. This was in response to an increasing number of problems involving large-scale trade, usually in wool or wine, over long distances and attempted to provide a speedier response to disputes.

London Bridge

In 1274 at his coronation feast (or in 1281, depending on which source you believe), the leaders of the City of London approached Edward, complaining about the poor state of London Bridge – it was, as the nursery rhyme states, 'falling down'!

The Londoners' complaint was that the taxes and rents raised from the houses and businesses on the bridge were meant to pay for the upkeep of the bridge. But, in 1269, Henry III had awarded them to his wife Eleanor and she had diverted the money into her own personal income.

In response, Edward assured the Corporation of the City of London that the bridge would be repaired, and the taxes redirected to its upkeep. There followed a huge row with his wife, but she was forced to relinquish the money. Edward was determined to be seen as fair to all his subjects and not, unlike his father, favour family over what he thought was his duty. He even awarded the Corporation the right to charge tolls to cross the bridge for three years in order to fund rebuilding costs.

SOURCE 4

London Bridge in the sixteenth century.

THINK

5 Do the actions by Edward outlined above show him following self-interest or enforcing good government?

THINK

1 To what extent did medieval kings rely on administrators like Burnell?
2 What does the life of Robert Burnell tell us about public service in the thirteenth century?
3 Do you think Edward was right to trust Burnell?

ACTIVITY

How significant was Robert Burnell?

There are several different ways to 'measure' the significance of something. We like to use the criteria below.

A person might be significant if they:

● changed events at the time they lived
● improved lots of people's lives – or made them worse
● changed people's ideas
● had a long-lasting impact on their country or the world
● set a really good or a very bad example to other people of how to live or behave.

If you have your own criteria, then feel free to use them for this activity.

1 Using these significance criteria how significant do you think Robert Burnell was during Edward's reign?
2 As you already know, views on significance can change over time. Someone who seemed to be significant in the 1270s might not appear as significant today. Would you regard Burnell as a significant person today?

Robert Burnell profile

Using the information on these two pages and your own research, write a short profile of Robert Burnell (in the style of the Profile on page 15) using no more than six bullet points.

Robert Burnell, Chancellor

Edward was ably supported by his officials, many of whom served him faithfully throughout his reign, although some, including Chief Justice Hengham, were dismissed for dishonesty in 1289. Perhaps the most important was Robert Burnell.

Burnell was born in Shropshire around 1239 into a 'middling' family. He became a clerk (a priest), which was probably the best way to get an EDUCATION at the time. We first come across him when he is employed in Prince Edward's household during the 1250s. How important he had become is shown by the fact that Burnell was one of five trustees named by Edward to run his affairs whilst he was on Crusade. When Edward returned as King in 1274, Burnell was immediately made his Chancellor, which was the most important administrative position in the government. Some historians describe it as being the equivalent of our modern-day prime minister. Burnell was almost always by Edward's side when decisions were made. He was immensely influential, and completely trusted by Edward.

The route to the king

Burnell was, above all else, supremely efficient. He reorganised the workings of the CHANCELLERY, keeping a tighter track of paperwork; and there was plenty of it. He was the driving force behind the Hundred Rolls enquiries, and took the lead in writing the Statute of Westminster. Burnell was responsible for ensuring that the Chancery and other parts of government business stayed in London rather than follow the King around the country. He made a point of being accessible to all, and appearing approachable, listening to complaints and, where possible, acting on them. He became the preferred route to the King. People wanting access to the King, or even just to explain their actions, would take up the matter with Burnell and trust him to take the appropriate action. All this made him even more indispensable to Edward and increased his power and influence.

A trusted diplomat

Although almost always at Edward's side, Burnell was used for delicate diplomacy. He went to Paris in 1286 to meet with the King of France and sort out problems over Edward paying homage to the French king for his lands in Gascony. Edward also sent him to Gascony in 1288 to reorganise government there.

Personal gain

There was a darker side to all this power and influence, however. Serving Edward made Robert Burnell extremely rich! By the time he died, in 1292, Burnell owned 82 manors in 19 counties. He traded in the debts of impoverished knights, and even loaned the King money – 3,000 marks in 1282, and again in 1285. He was awarded multiple LIVINGS by Edward, being made the priest in more than one parish. He collected the income from each parish but paid a curate a small fee to take all the services for him. This was lucrative, and quite common in medieval times, but against Church law. In 1269 Edward granted him the right to hold a weekly market in his home town of Acton Burnell, and two annual fairs. Edward managed to make Burnell Bishop of Bath and Wells in 1275, where he used his own money to rebuild the Great Hall there.

Edward tried to have Burnell elected Archbishop of Canterbury in 1270 and again in 1278, and Bishop of Winchester in 1280, both very lucrative livings. On each occasion, Edward was unable to persuade the Pope to support Burnell, partly because of his morals. Despite being a cleric and therefore supposedly CELIBATE, Robert Burnell had a mistress called Juliana and several illegitimate children.

He died in 1292 and was buried in the nave of Wells Cathedral; but his heart was buried in Bath Abbey.

Acton Burnell Castle: What does his house tell us about Robert Burnell?

The Burnell family had lived in Acton Burnell from the 1180s. Robert inherited half of the manor. He was given permission by Edward I in 1284 to fortify the new home he was building to replace the much smaller house he had been born in. He was given a dozen oak trees from the royal forest to help build it. The new castle was built from local red sandstone, and designed to reflect the importance of its owner. He also built the adjacent church. Robert's wealth allowed him to employ the best masons, and use the best materials! Acton Burnell, situated in the Welsh Marches, was central to Edward's plans to conquer Wales (see pages 54–60) and so he was a frequent visitor to the castle.

Acton Burnell is what we call a fortified manor house rather than a castle. One look at the building suggests that it was not designed for defence, but as a comfortable place to live. It is said to be the finest still standing in England. It tells us a lot about the status of its owner, one of the most powerful men in England.

The fact Robert built a fortified manor house rather than a castle also tells us about life in England at the time – Edward may have been trying to subdue the Welsh but in England life was thought to be much more settled – there was less need for strong walls to keep out attackers! Parliament met in Acton Burnell twice: in 1283 and 1285. In 1283 it met in the nearby tithe barn, and in 1285 in the (still unfinished) house. The house was incomplete when Robert died in 1292.

THINK

4   Look carefully at the photograph and the floor plan (Sources 5 and 6) and pick out the features that suggest the primary purpose of Acton Burnell Castle was as somewhere to live, rather than somewhere to be safe.

5   Look carefully at Source 5. How is Acton Burnell Castle similar to, and different from, a typical Norman 'motte and bailey' castle?

6   What statement about Robert Burnell is this house designed to make?

SOURCE 5

Acton Burnell Castle as it is today.

FIGURE 6

Floor plan of the first floor of Acton Burnell Castle, produced by English Heritage.

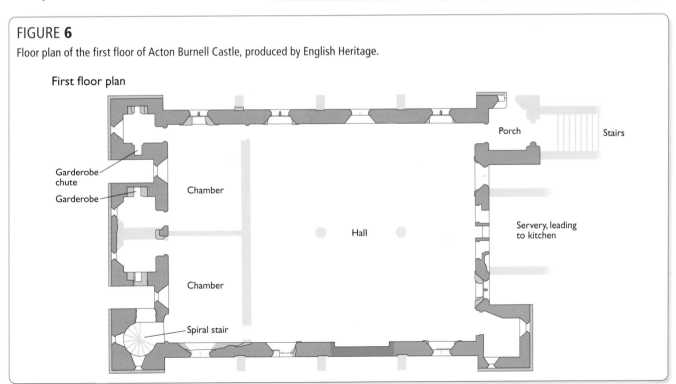

First floor plan

Garderobe chute

Garderobe

Chamber

Chamber

Spiral stair

Hall

Porch   Stairs

Servery, leading to kitchen

The development of Parliament

Under Edward, Parliament tended to meet twice a year, in Spring and in Autumn. It was really an extension of the King's Council, his chief advisors like Robert Burnell and the main barons. In fact it was often composed of whoever was around at the time a decision needed to be made! Meetings at Christmas and Easter would be larger, and gradually the principle evolved that the King should ask for advice when major decisions needed to be made from as large a group as possible. This led on to specially-convened meetings of Parliament ('parler' is the French verb for 'to talk') where the King would listen to what those present had to say, although he was under no obligation whatsoever to act on that advice if he disagreed.

How Parliament worked

Agendas were fluid, and initially no formal records were kept. Business was whatever the Crown found convenient at that time. Much discussion under Edward was on granting him a tax, either to pay off his debts or, later in his reign, to pay for wars with Wales and Scotland. Often it was difficult to persuade Parliament to grant a tax, or they would expect redress of grievances in exchange. Many of these were presented as petitions, and in the early part of Edward's reign, Parliament seemed to spend more time dealing with petitions than anything else. These might be from individuals, or from guilds of merchants or towns. The response of Parliament might, in effect, change the law or the interpretation of the law, hence the beginning of the idea that Parliament should make law.

The King would often use Parliament as a sounding board, or a place to try out ideas for legislation or change, and use the response of Parliament to gauge the possible impact on the country as a whole. Something totally unpopular might be withdrawn rather than provoke antagonism. But many of Edward's actions trying to restore royal authority met with a strong response, he still maintained he had the right to re-assert ROYAL PREROGATIVE.

Earls, barons and bishops were always summoned in person to Parliament, although in the early years we do not know how many attended. There are records of those who witness charters, government decrees and the like but how representative these names are we cannot tell. Edward invited burgesses from the towns and knights from the shires (the 'commons') when business warranted it or when he wanted their approval for a tax or to go to war. We have already seen that he invited around 800 people to the Parliament of 1275. Edward wanted approval for his actions from as wide a circle of society as possible. By the end of his reign, the barons were trying to enforce what they saw as proper conduct by the King through Parliament, thus using Parliament in their conflicts with the King.

SOURCE 7

A sixteenth-century illustration of Edward I presiding over Parliament in 1300. The scene shows Alexander III of Scotland and Llywelyn ap Gruffudd of Wales on either side of Edward – an episode that never actually occurred.

THINK

1   What did Edward want from Parliament?
2   What did the Lords and 'commons' want from Parliament?

Edward's 'Model Parliament' of 1295

In 1295 Edward was faced with a war with France and Scotland. To fight this he needed money. The only way he could raise the amounts needed was by the approval of Parliament, which Edward duly summoned (see Source 8).

SOURCE 8

A Writ of Summons to Parliament for the county of Northampton.

The King to the sheriff of Northampton, greeting. Whereas we wish to have a conference and discussion with the earls, barons and other nobles of our realm concerning the provision of remedies for the dangers that in these days threaten the same kingdom – on which account we have ordered them to come to us at Westminster on the Sunday next after the feast of St Martin in the coming winter, there to consider, ordain, and do whatever the avoidance of such dangers may demand – we command and firmly enjoin you that without delay you cause two knights, of the more discreet and more capable of labour, to be elected from the aforesaid county, and two citizens from each city of the aforesaid county, and two burgesses from each borough, and that you have them come to us on the day and at the place aforesaid; so that the said knights shall then and there have full and sufficient authority on behalf of themselves and the community of the county aforesaid, and the said citizens and burgesses on behalf of themselves and the respective communities of the cities and borough aforesaid, to do whatever in the aforesaid matters may be ordained by common counsel; and so that, through default of such authority the aforesaid business shall by no means remain unfinished. And you are there to have the names of the knights, citizens, and burgesses together with this writ. By witness of the King, at Canterbury.

Edward used the phrase, 'What touches all should be approved by all,' when summoning this Parliament, and this led to the inclusion of the lower clergy too. One proctor (representative of the clergy) was summoned from every cathedral in the country, and two from each diocese. Edward hoped to be granted a tax to fight, and he got one, reluctantly, but much less than he asked for. The Lords voted him one-eleventh of their income, the clergy one-tenth (they also established the principle that taxing the clergy needed the approval of the Pope), and boroughs and towns agreed one-seventh. It was barely enough to pay for a war, and it did set the precedent that only Parliament could vote taxes to the King. It was also the first occasion when the Commons (knights and burgesses) met separately from the Lords, so perhaps that too is why this is known as the MODEL PARLIAMENT. The members knew they had the King firmly in their grasp as he desperately needed money for war and so was in little position to argue.

FOCUS TASK B

In what ways did Parliament change during Edward's reign? Part 2

You have been creating a diagram showing how Parliament changed under Edward.

1 Which of the changes you have noted was **most** important in your view.
2 Use your diagram to write an account of how Parliament changed under Edward.

TOPIC SUMMARY

The development of government, rights and justice

- Edward spent a lot of time and energy trying to restore royal rights and prerogatives.
- He also tried hard to remedy injustices that were brought to his attention, including, if necessary, replacing royal officials.
- England was administered more efficiently in 1290 than in 1274 – Edward placed a lot of emphasis on 'good government'.
- Edward's incessant need for money allowed Parliament to develop a more formal and powerful role, especially later in his reign.
- Historians are divided in their opinion of Edward's motives for many of his actions.

THINK

Read Source 8 carefully.

3 Who is Edward inviting to Parliament? How is this different to most parliaments?
4 What does Edward mean by 'have full and sufficient authority ... to do whatever ... may be ordained'?
5 Why might historians call this a 'Model Parliament'?
6 To what extent would a modern-day Member of Parliament recognise Edward I's parliament?

DEBATE

How powerful was Parliament?

- Because, in 1265, he invited the Commons to Parliament to support him against the Barons, Simon de Montfort has become known as the 'Father of Parliament'.
- According to Prestwich, *Edward I* (1997), Edward's first Parliament, in 1275, was the largest ever held in the Middle Ages, and was designed to negotiate a tax on trade, as much as to assert his authority.
- In 1295, according to Raban, (2000) at the so-called 'Model Parliament' Edward invited the lower clergy as well as people from the towns and counties, using the phrase, 'what touches all should be approved by all'.
- By the end of his reign Edward's ability to wage war was severely restricted by Parliament's reluctance to grant taxation for the purpose.

KEY WORDS

Make sure you know what these terms mean:
- Feudal system
- Model parliament
- Rights
- Justice
- Statute
- Corruption
- Burgesses

REVIEW OF CHAPTER 1

Government: the rights of King and people

What kind of king was Edward I?

Look back at the introduction to this book, and especially the answer you wrote to the Focus Task question, 'What kind of king will Edward be?'. You are now going to review that answer in the light of the work you have completed in Chapter 1.

Part 1

Here is our list of what people expected of a medieval king:

- To defend the country
- To produce an heir
- To keep the law
- To protect the Church
- To ensure that people can live their daily lives in safety and freedom

1 Which of these aspects of kingship have been dealt with in Chapter 1?
2 How well do you think Edward has dealt with these aspects of kingship?

Part 2

Below is a blank 'living graph' plus a list of key events or actions covered in this chapter.

On your own copy of this graph place each event above or below the line, depending on how far this shows Edward acting in his own self-interest, or in the interests of his people and 'good government'. The higher or lower you place an event, the stronger it fits that descriptor.

It is possible that an action is in **both** Edward's and the people's interest. If so it should appear twice - both above and below the line. But **how far above** and **how far below** will show how you think the balance falls between Edward's interests and the people's interests.

For example, 'repairs to London Bridge in 1281' might be in the best interests of the people because lots of people in London used it to cross the river. But it might also be argued that repairing the bridge was in Edward's best interests, because he wanted to keep the support of the rich leaders of the City of London.

There is no one correct answer to any of these issues! You just have to be sure that you have evidence to support your judgement. So for each item you place add a short explanation for your placing – supporting it with evidence from the chapter.

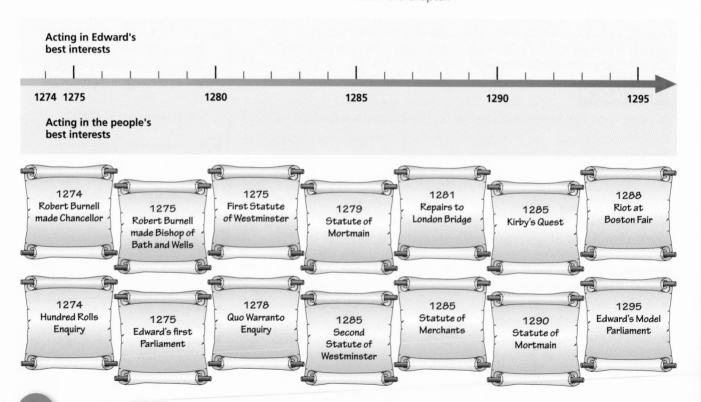

Acting in Edward's best interests

1274 1275   1280   1285   1290   1295

Acting in the people's best interests

1274 Robert Burnell made Chancellor

1275 Robert Burnell made Bishop of Bath and Wells

1275 First Statute of Westminster

1279 Statute of Mortmain

1281 Repairs to London Bridge

1285 Kirby's Quest

1288 Riot at Boston Fair

1274 Hundred Rolls Enquiry

1275 Edward's first Parliament

1278 Quo Warranto Enquiry

1285 Second Statute of Westminster

1285 Statute of Merchants

1290 Statute of Mortmain

1295 Edward's Model Parliament

Practice questions

It is a good idea to use practice questions to review your learning. In your exam you will be set four questions on the British depth study.

Question 1 will be 'an interpretation question'. You will need to use your knowledge to explain how convincing the interpretation is. The interpretation could be written or visual. For example:

> ### INTERPRETATION A
>
> A R.F. Treherne, in his book *Baronial Plan of Reform*, describing Edward.
>
> *Edward was no more than an irresponsible, arrogant and headstrong boy, treacherously selfish in the heedless pursuit of his own ends, indulging in every whim at his own pleasure, and incapable of self-discipline or obedience to external authority in anything that conflicted with the passions and hatreds of the moment.*

> 1. How convincing is Interpretation A about Edward's character?
>   (8 marks)

For this question you should aim to describe what you can see and then use detailed knowledge to support and contradict what the source tells you about Edward's crusade. Try to find at least three points on either side – convincing and not convincing.

Use the questions below to help you get started.

- What are Treherne's criticisms of Edward?
- Is Treherne talking about Edward as king, or Edward as prince?
- Do the points Treherne makes agree with other evidence in this chapter?
- Do the points Treherne makes agree with your own view of Edward?

Question 2 will ask you to 'explain' something – for example some development or change in the period. It is testing your knowledge and understanding. For example:

> 2. Explain what was important about the new statutes Edward passed during his reign.
>   (8 marks)

There are many things you could cover but you should focus on those that show the importance of the statutes not the incidental details.

1   Which of the following do you think you should spend most time on?
- they addressed complaints made to the King
- they dealt with salmon fishing
- they made the country fairer and safer
- they made people feel more involved in government
- they showed Edward to be a caring king

2   Look back at Topic 1.2 to see how you could expand on your chosen point.

Question 3 asks you to write an account. This is a 'narrative' question, testing your knowledge and understanding and analysis of historical events. For example:

> 3. Write an account of the ways Parliament changed under Edward I.
>   (8 marks)

For this question you should cover a range of events and developments with enough detail to show you understand the different stages in the development of Parliament and how they are connected. You could include:

- composition of Parliament
- regularity of meeting
- taking advice from those present
- not just about granting the King money/taxes
- became more critical of the King as time went on.

Use your work on Topic 1.2 (particularly the Focus Task on page 16) to write a paragraph on at least two of these points. You should aim to connect them together to show changes in order to reflect the focus of the question which is about 'change'.

Question 4 will be on the historic environment. You will be given a statement about the period and will be asked to reach a judgement on how far a historical site you have studied supports the statement. You should be balanced and analytical but the key will be to make a judgement about how far the statement is true and to write a coherent essay to back up your judgement.

We don't know which site you will study as it changes every year but you can practice with any site. One of the sites you have studied in this chapter is Acton Burnell (see page 18) the home of Chancellor Robert Burnell, which is one of the best examples of a fortified manor house from this period.

> 4. 'The main change Edward I brought to England was good government.' How far does a study of Acton Burnell Castle support this statement.
>   (16 marks)

Read the information on pages 18–19 about the castle and its owner Robert Burnell and use it plan an answer to two or three of these questions.

- Who was Robert Burnell?
- How typical was he of rich people in Edward's England?
- Why did he build Acton Burnell?
- Does the house look more like a home or a castle?
- What does that tell you about the state of England at the time?

Life in medieval England

2

In this picture from a medieval manuscript, the farmers are carefully looking after their sheep. One is being milked. Another is being treated with some kind of medicine. You can tell from this picture how important sheep were in medieval England. In fact, England depended on them. There were more sheep than people. Sheep, or at least the wool they produced, were the basis of England's growing wealth.

Many other things were changing in England too. Some people argue that the changes in England during this period were as fundamental as those of the Industrial Revolution in the eighteenth and nineteenth centuries.

This chapter examines various aspects of medieval England:
- working life in towns and villages and how it was changing;
- the role of the Church and especially its role in education and learning
- the legal system and how Edward tried to restore law and order after the chaos of Henry III's reign.

How wealthy was England in 1300?

In 1966, ARCHAEOLOGISTS excavating in Southampton uncovered the remains of a merchant's house, probably the house of Richard of Southwick. His seal, and that of another merchant, were found on the site. During the excavations, they found some finely painted wine-jugs (see Source 1) from south-west France; glazed pottery from Spain; glass from Venice; silk from Persia; and wooden vessels, preserved in the waterlogged soil, from the Low Countries and the Baltic region. The windows in his house were glazed, the floors tiled, and the drain was stone-lined. He even kept a pet Barbary ape! Other debris from a cesspit showed that he ate very well indeed, including imported fruit such as pomegranates, figs and oranges. This find confirms how extensive England's international trading links were in 1300.

There is also much evidence of internal trade at this time. In 1291 we find coal being shipped from Newcastle to Corfe Castle in Dorset, and to London in 1305. The rebuilding of English cathedrals at this time, in itself an indication of how wealthy England was, consumed huge quantities of Purbeck marble. Tin from Cornwall was in great demand around Europe. And the merchants of the CINQUE PORTS were licensed by the King to fish for herrings off the east coast of England in the late summer and autumn, landing most of their catch at Yarmouth. This trade was organised by merchants like Richard of Southwick, and depended on having a reliable network of contacts, sometimes family members, at stages along the trade route. They also depended on being able to borrow money. Central to this were the Italian bankers, some of whom had set up offices in London sometime before 1300.

SOURCE 1

Saintonge jug from Gascony, south-west France, found in excavations of the merchant's house in Cuckoo Lane, Southampton, 1966.

The wool trade

But the most important trade of all was the wool trade to Europe. Each year around 40,000 sacks of wool were exported. Isabella de Fortibus, for example, had over 7,000 sheep grazing on eleven different manors in and around Holderness, near the River Humber. Each year from 1260 to 1280 she sold their wool for at least £200, an immense sum at that time, to just one company, the Riccardi of Lucca in Italy.

It was not surprising that as a sign of his status, the Lord Chancellor sat on the 'Woolsack' in the House of Lords. It was the wool trade that was the driving force behind overseas trade, and created the wealth to allow merchants to import luxuries like those found in Richard's house in Southampton.

THINK

1   Study Source 1. Do you think this jug was for everyday use or for special occasions?
2   What do the items found in the remains of Richard of Southwick's house tell us about: a) his wealth, b) Southampton activities and c) England around 1300?
3   Study Figure 2. Make a list of any of the goods that you are not familiar with, carry out some research and write a definition of each.
4   How different is the picture of England described here, compared with the one you discovered in Year 7?
5   Do you think England was a wealthy country in 1300?

FIGURE 2

Map showing England's main trade links by 1300.

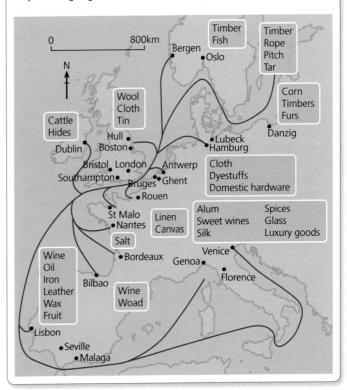

2.1 Trade, towns and villages

FOCUS TASK

Winners and losers in Edward's England. Part 1

As you study this topic note down examples of people (individuals or groups) who either gained or lost from the social changes taking place in the reign of Edward I.

FOCUS

By 1290 England had experienced 30 years of continuous good harvests. The population had doubled or possibly trebled from the time of the Norman invasion. The country was developing a CASH ECONOMY. More people lived in towns than ever before. As we have seen, England was fully integrated into the economy of Europe, and it appeared Europe had an insatiable desire for high quality English wool. But new wealth also brought tensions within society. This topic explores some of these changes.

How was agriculture changing?
The story of Hugh Cok

In 1277 Hugh Cok had been the poorest peasant in the village of Codicote, in Hertfordshire. By the time of his death in 1306 he left quite an ESTATE to his daughter, Christina. Part of the reason for his success is that he seems to have been a wise and determined businessman. He rented a stall in the local market to sell fish, which was much in demand because there were three meat-free days each week (Wednesday, Friday and Saturday) by order of the Church. Other times of the year, such as Lent, were meant to be meat-free too. Cok was so successful over the next few years that he was able to buy or rent eight separate small pieces of land. He later rented another strip of land for ten years and another for four. The income from these pieces of land allowed him to buy a plot and then build a new house for himself and his family. In time, he bought another piece of land and hedged it, so he had his own ENCLOSED field rather than having some strips in a shared open field. He leased yet more land for twelve years, and also brewed beer. We know this because he was fined in the Manor Court for brewing bad beer!

Hugh's success was unusual, however, it illustrates some important changes taking place in English villages, particularly changes in the feudal system.

A cash economy

England was becoming a cash economy. Instead of depending on the feudal system (in which Lords of the Manor granted land to villagers and got labour services in return) many landowners now preferred to rent out their land for cash and to pay wages to peasants. Often 50 per cent of a land owners' income might be cash from these rents. Open fields and common land were being enclosed by landowners so they could graze sheep.

THINK

1 What does the story of Hugh Cok tell us about village life in Edward I's time?
2 Compare the farming carried out by Hugh Cok with what you know about medieval farming from your previous history courses. What are the similarities and differences? How can you explain any differences?
3 Why do you think Lords of the Manor preferred to rent out land, rather than rely on free labour from the peasants?
4 Write a new caption for Source 1 which explains how this aspect of village life was changing.

SOURCE 1

The village reeve, or Lord of the Manor's official, supervising the harvest.

For the peasants this meant more opportunity for some but poverty and hardship for others. In 1300 a quarter of rural families rented or owned enough land to support themselves, however, the rest did not. Many had no land at all. They had to work for wages to earn enough to buy food to feed their families or to earn money in others ways. For example:

- Brewing ale and selling it in the village was commonly carried out by women supplementing the family income.
- Increasingly, cash crops were produced – milk, eggs and cheese, fruit and vegetables, honey and wax for candles which were sold in the growing towns.
- Hemp and MADDER were produced for the cloth trade.

One effect of these changes was that countryside and town were increasingly integrated. Many new markets were set up in the late 1200s (by 1300 there were around 1,500). Increasingly, trades such as pottery making and cloth making, which had been village based, were spreading to towns.

Meanwhile, in the villages:

- More animals meant more manure and that meant more crops.
- Windmills started to make an appearance, supplementing existing watermills.
- Horses were replacing oxen for ploughing and for carting.

The wool trade

The biggest driver of change was the wool trade. Wool was making England wealthy. English wool was seen as the best in Europe so was in great demand by cloth makers. The result was that by 1300 there were an estimated 12 million sheep in England and most of these were raised and kept by ordinary villagers. Dyer, in his book *Making a Living in the Middle Ages*, estimates that 66 per cent of all wool produced in England came from small flocks averaging around twenty sheep owned by peasants.

There was more to the wool industry than just grazing sheep. From fleece to cloth this growing industry involved many different people and trades as summarised in the diagram below.

THINK

1 Which job would you most have liked to have in the wool trade?

Turning the wool into cloth involved many more people. In the thirteenth century this work was mostly done in Flanders but in the fourteenth century this part of the process took place increasingly in England.

- **Spinners** and **carders** turned the fleece into thread.
- **Fullers** softened the wool or the cloth. They had to trample the wool in urine all day.
- **Dyers** coloured the wool or cloth. Farmers supplied the plants needed for dyeing the wool.
- **Weavers** needed a fast hand and a careful eye. Their work was the final link in the chain that turned raw wool into high-quality cloth fit for the homes and clothes of rich nobles and merchants.

Shepherds: You would need to love sheep for this job – lambing in the dead of night in the middle of winter or searching for lost sheep on a hillside in the pouring rain. You might also need to go to market to buy ruddle for marking the sheep or to sell or buy sheep.

Builders were needed to make or repair the buildings that housed the sheep through the winter.

Clerks kept a record of how many sheep were in the flock and how much wool there would be to sell. Clerks had to be able to read, write and count – these were rare skills in those days.

Each spring the sheep were sheared. **Shearers** needed strong arms and a steady hand.

Merchants: Landlords or monasteries would often deal directly with an export merchant who would agree in advance a price for their wool. Peasants were more likely to take their wool to market to get the best price.

Administrators: The growing trade needed good organisers to keep everything running smoothly!

Sailors: Most of the wool went to Flanders to be made into cloth. Sailors loaded the wool sacks onto ships to Bruges and Ghent. Sailors needed good sea legs and had to be ready to fight off pirates.

Packers: Wool was loaded into sacks and transported long distances by donkey to ports such as London, Southampton and Boston. Packers needed to protect their cargo from thieves.

Town life

Towns were changing too. One effect of the changes in the villages was that an increasing number of people moved to towns looking for opportunities. If you could live in the town for a year and a day without being taken back to your village, you became a FREEMAN. Alternatively, many Lords would now allow surplus workers to leave the manor and go to town in exchange for payment of a fine. It was usually younger people or landless labourers who headed for towns, although sometimes rural craftsmen would move to have a bigger market for their goods.

Buying and selling

Markets were the reason towns grew. The main street of the town would be lined by merchants' houses, and would lead into the market place, where there would be stalls selling goods of every description. There might even be acrobats, musicians or bear-baiting going on (see Source 4), pie sellers shouting their wares, urchins demanding to look after your horse, watch your goods, or lead you to an inn or a tavern. There might be sheep or poultry for sale – it would be very noisy and busy!

Towns weren't just a place to buy and sell; they were places to make things too. In the relatively small town of Coventry in the thirteenth century, for example, you would find people working in the cloth and woollen trades, or leather and fur trades. There you would find people brewing and selling ale and wine. You would find carpenters, metal workers, wheelwrights, fletchers, bow-string makers, basket makers, wig makers, parchment makers, charcoal burners, turners, scribes, coopers and carters. You might even find locksmiths, glove makers, tailors, millers and ropemakers. No wonder towns were attracting so many more people.

New towns

During Edward I's reign, many new towns were established by the King, Lords of the Manor and the Church. Successful towns were seen as a good way to make money from rents, tolls and land sales.

Kingston upon Hull, as it became known, is perhaps the best example from the time. The town of Wyke had been set up by the monastery of Meaux and become moderately successful – it had grown to have a population of 60 households. When Edward bought it from the monks in 1293, he immediately improved the roads to and from the town, granted it permission to hold two weekly markets and an annual fair. By 1299 Hull had its own charter, its own court, prison and gallows, and its merchants were exempt from tolls throughout the whole country. Hull grew rapidly and became a successful port for the export of wool to Europe.

SOURCE 2

A medieval merchant's house, built in the 1290s by John Fortin, a prosperous merchant. It was restored in the 1980s and still stands in Southampton, run as a tourist attraction by English Heritage.

Living conditions

You would smell a medieval town long before you could see it! Approaching medieval Exeter, for example, you had to cross what was known as Shitebrook, the stream where the *gongfleurs* or NIGHT SOIL MEN dumped the sewage they had collected that night.

The next thing you would notice is the church, cathedral or castle dominating the skyline. Large towns or cities would normally be surrounded by a wall. Coventry built a wall around the city (it took them 100 years to build it!), not for defence, but to emphasise its own importance. You would enter the town through one of the gates – in that way non-residents could easily be charged tolls for using bridges, selling in the market, and so on, and residents could keep an eye on strangers. At dusk the gates would be closed.

Poor people were squeezed into older houses hidden away from the centre. Landlords built houses to rent: John de Cardiff, a Bristol merchant, was earning £22 per year just in rent from houses he owned in the city.

There were many threats to health. Infectious diseases could spread quickly in the overcrowded conditions. It was difficult to get fresh water to drink. Richard of Southwick (page 25) may have had a stone-lined drain, but most people did not.

Yet efforts *were* made to clean up towns. In Lincoln, in 1286, pavements were laid along the main streets, NOXIOUS TRADES, such as tanning and butchering animals, were gradually moved to the edges of towns as, by 1300, were many animal markets. Town governments made efforts to clear the streets and from time to time limit the number of pigs roaming about. People often made great efforts to wash and keep clean. Mutton fat, wood ash or potash, and natural soda were used to make soap for washing both people and clothes. Rich people could afford Castile soap, imported from Spain and made from olive oil. If you had servants, they had the job of heating enough water to fill the bath, and to dispose of the dirty water afterwards.

SOURCE 3

Having a bath, medieval style, from a contemporary illuminated manuscript.

THINK

5 Which of the pictures on these two pages do you find most helpful in understanding what life was like in a medieval town? Give your reasons.

SOURCE 4

A modern interpretation of a medieval fair.

SOURCE 5

Street entertainment, medieval style, from a fourteenth-century illuminated manuscript.

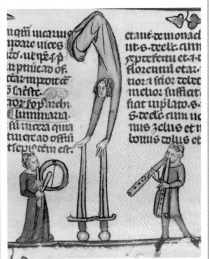

SOURCE 6

Edward's Italian bankers at work in 1294.

SOURCE 7

Making coins by hand in medieval times. Note the hammer used to strike the silver into a die in order to make the coin.

SOURCE 8

Groat coin (4d) from Edward's re-coinage.

THINK

1 Study Source 8. Why might Edward want his image on his coins?
2 Why is there a cross on the reverse?
3 What motives did Edward have for issuing new coins?

Royal finance and taxation

Edward I was always short of money. You have already studied in Chapter 1 how he returned from his Crusade deeply in debt and how Parliament was often reluctant to vote him a tax. So he had to find other ways to make money.

Taxing the wool trade

In 1272, the export of wool to Flanders was banned because of a dispute between the two countries. However merchants were desperate to sell their wool. They approached Edward, asking him to settle the dispute. As part of this settlement the wool merchants agreed to pay Edward a CUSTOMS DUTY of 7s 6d on every sack of wool exported through London and thirteen other ports. This was RATIFIED by Edward's first Parliament meeting in 1275.

Borrowing from his bankers

Even before he became King, Edward depended on the Riccardi family of Lucca for loans (see Source 6). They partly funded his Crusade. When he became King he borrowed money from them using the customs duties on wool mentioned above as security. Edward's Welsh wars (see pages 54–6) were largely financed by such loans.

It is estimated that by 1294 Edward had borrowed a total of over £390,000 from the Riccardi family. But in 1294 it all went wrong. When war broke out with France, the Riccardis were caught short of funds, as they were financing the King of France, as well as Edward. Communications were disrupted between England and Italy and the bank didn't have enough cash to meet the demands on it. Angry at their lack of funds and their support for France, Edward DEFAULTED on his debts and the Riccardi were ruined. Other Italian banks, including the Frescobaldi family, took over and became Edward's main source of loans until his death. Bankers were always willing to lend to Edward because of the security provided by the customs duty on, and the strong demand for, English wool.

Edward's new coinage

At the start of Edward's reign the only coins in circulation were silver pennies. If you wanted a half-penny, you would literally cut a penny in half. However there were problems with the coinage. Some people clipped coins (shaved some extra silver off them) although this was a serious crime. There were also lots of under-value French coins circulating in England – coins which did not contain enough silver. England was becoming a cash economy and a cash economy needs coins that everyone trusts so Edward took action.

- One royal MONEYER, Philip de Cambio, was arrested and charged with issuing coins with not enough silver in them. He was found guilty and hanged.
- All the goldsmiths and Jewish moneylenders in the country were arrested and charged with COIN-CLIPPING. A total of 273 JEWS were found guilty and hanged.
- In 1279 Edward agreed to call in all existing coins and replace them with new ones, bearing his image. He then borrowed £20,000 SILVER BULLION from his Italian bankers and began minting new coins. New values were introduced: the groat, worth 4d, the halfpenny and the farthing, so no one needed to clip coins any more. As the old coins were collected and replaced, they were melted down and made into new ones. The whole process created a profit of £25,000 for Edward.

Wool tax

The Statute of Merchants 1285 (see Chapter 1, page 19) was designed to deal specifically with disputes between merchants over contracts, payments for goods and the like – the very bedrock of successful trade. But in 1294, faced with the prospect of war with both Scotland and France and a desperate need for quick funds, Edward decided to raise the wool tax to a whopping 40s per sack. Most of the rich wool merchants agreed to this, after all they could just pass on the cost to customers by charging more. However, many others resisted. Wool prices were at a low, and so a 40s tax was an enormous demand. The Lords stated in Parliament that 'the whole country feels itself burdened by the tax on wools, which is excessively burdensome, for the wool of England amounts to almost the value of half of the whole land'. As we have seen, many people, peasants, small landowners, great landowners, churches and monasteries depended on wool, and on selling their wool at a fair price. Opposition spread and in 1296 the tax was removed, only to be re-imposed in 1303, but only on foreign, not English, merchants.

Laurence of Ludlow was one of the richest wool merchants in the country and had agreed to the tax. He was drowned off the coast of England in 1294 on his way to Flanders to sell wool the King had seized from foreign merchants and the Riccardi for him. On announcing his death, the Chronicler of Dunstable Priory wrote, 'He it was who induced the merchants of England to grant the King 40s for each sack of wool … and because he sinned against the wool suppliers, he was drowned in a ship laden with wool.' There is no need to add that Dunstable Priory obtained most of its wealth from the wool trade!

> **THINK**
>
> 4 Study Source 9. What does this contemporary illustration tell us about travelling by sea?
> 5 How useful is it as a source about Ludlow's death?
> 6 How convincing is it for telling us about the wool trade?
> 7 What might it tell us about how people thought of Laurence of Ludlow?

SOURCE 9

Laurence of Ludlow drowning, from the 'Chronica Maiora', thirteenth-century manuscript.
© The Master and Fellows of Corpus Christi College, Cambridge.

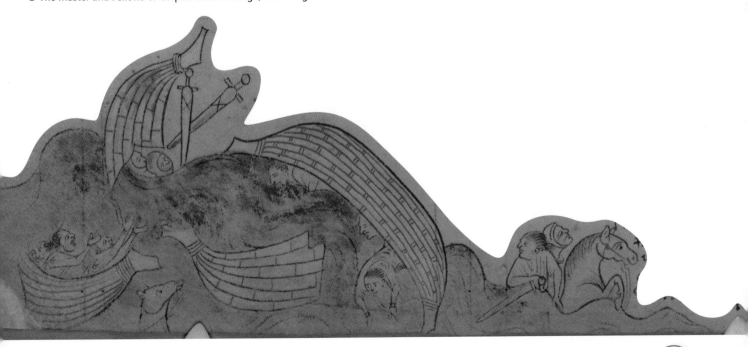

Stokesay Castle, a merchant's home

Stokesay Castle was the home of Laurence of Ludlow whose death was shown in Source 10 on page 31. Laurence of Ludlow, like his father before him, was an English wool merchant based in Shrewsbury, Shropshire.

From 1272 he traded wool from the area, and Wales, sending it all over Europe. He had an office in London, and is known to have regularly visited Ghent and Bruges, in the Low Countries, and Champagne in France – the biggest sheep fair in Europe at the time. He was wealthy enough to loan money to King Edward, and the Bishop of Worcester for rebuilding his cathedral, as well as many of the 'Marcher Lords' (see page 9) in the neighbourhood.

In 1281 he bought the Manor of Stokesay, along with 120 acres of arable land; six acres of meadow; a wood and two watermills. He immediately set about building a house reflecting his status and wealth (see Source 11). His wealth allowed him to employ the best craftsmen available at the time, and use the best materials. Perhaps that is why so much of the house remains today. It is perhaps the earliest known example in England of a wealthy merchant moving to the country and becoming a landed gentleman.

When it was built, Stokesay was not called a castle, rather it was called a manor house. You should be able to work out why: the Great Hall is obviously designed to be lived in, and to impress, and there is a solar (a private room for the homeowner and their family) at one end. A private place for the family to live, eat and sleep away from everyone in the castle was a new innovation. The large glazed windows of the Great Hall are designed to let in the maximum amount of light during the day rather than for defence.

SOURCE 10

Calendar of patent rolls, 1291, Oct 19, Hereford.

Licence for Lawrence de Lodelawe to strengthen his dwelling-house of Stok Say, co. Salop, with a wall of stone and lime, and to crenellate the same.

THINK

1 How can you tell this drawing (Source 11) shows the house around 1290?
2 How is Stokesay similar to, and different from, a typical motte and bailey castle?
3 Which features of the house are designed for protection?
4 What does that tell us about life in Shropshire and the Marcher Lands at the time?

SOURCE 11

A modern drawing, by English Heritage, showing Stokesay Castle in about 1290.

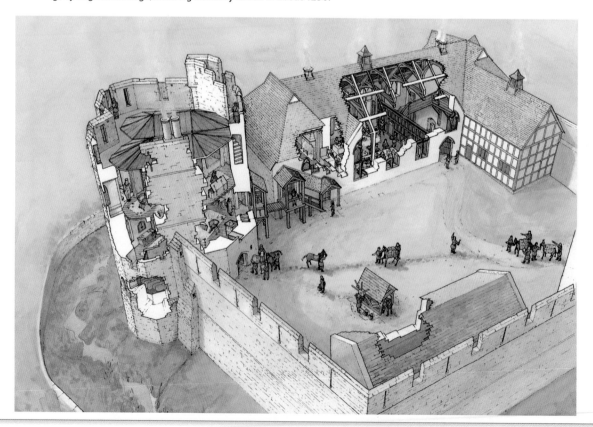

By 1283 Edward had conquered Wales (see Chapter 3, pages 54–6) and thus life was becoming much more settled in the Marcher lands bordering Wales. Perhaps that is what encouraged Laurence to buy his estate and build his house. But, and this is a big but, however wealthy he had become, he would not dare anger the barons of the area by building a castle, which might seem to challenge their authority. Hence the design of the house had more to do with showing off his wealth rather than asserting authority.

SOURCE 12

Stokesay Castle as it is today.

SOURCE 13

Inside the Great Hall at Stokesay Castle today.

THINK

5   What does Stokesay Castle tell us about the wool trade?
6   What does it tell us about Laurence of Ludlow?
7   Do you think Stokesay Castle could have been built in the 1260s?

Subsequent history of Stokesay Castle

Most of what you can see of Stokesay Castle today dates from the end of the thirteenth century. But there have been a few changes since. During the English Civil War, the CURTAIN WALLS were pulled down and the moat filled in. (No one is even sure if the moat ever contained water.) A new gate house was built around 1640, and there was some restoration in the eighteenth and nineteenth centuries, but very little documentation has survived telling us about the castle: the building itself is the biggest story-teller of all. The top quality of the building materials used tells us about Laurence's amazing wealth, which was all dependent on the wool trade.

Why did Edward expel all Jews from England in 1290?

In 1290 Edward made an order to EXPEL all Jews from England. In some ways this was a surprising action since he had depended greatly on Jewish money and taxes. To explain why he did this we need to look at some longer term factors as well as some short term causes.

Long-term developments

Royal finance

The first recorded Jews in England arrived in 1070, when William the Conqueror invited some Jews from Rouen to England to help with the royal finances. After this Jews quickly became indispensable to English monarchs. Henry III, for example, borrowed huge sums of money from them but he also taxed them for around £250,000 during his reign.

The Christian Church banned lending money for interest, so Jewish moneylenders filled that role. Landowners and merchants borrowed money from Jewish moneylenders for example to pay debts to the King; to buy land; even to go on a PILGRIMAGE or crusade. The borrowers developed a love–hate relationship with the lenders. They needed their money but they despised being in debt to them.

Religious differences

At a time when religion played such a large part in people's lives, the Jews became a target for hatred. They spoke a different language, dressed and behaved differently, and didn't attend church. They had their own services and their own beliefs that were widely misunderstood by Christians. They were required to wear a yellow badge on their outer clothes, showing two stone tablets which clearly identified them as being Jewish.

They were also blamed for crucifying Christ and out of this a particularly dangerous myth grew up known as the 'Blood Libel'. In 1144 a young boy named William was found dead in Norwich and the Jews were blamed for his death. The rumour spread that every year at Easter Jews crucified a young boy from a different town or city across Europe. They used the boy's blood as part of their services. It was pure myth but it was widely believed.

> **THINK**
>
> 1 Look closely at Source 14. Can you identify:
>   a) the merchants
>   b) the King
>   c) the Jews?
> 2 What do you think the person drawing the cartoon thinks about Jews? How can you tell?

SOURCE 14

A cartoon found on a list of tax payments by Jews in Norwich in 1233.

Short-term causes

By the time Edward I became king there were around 5,000 Jews living in England. Most were moneylenders, although some traded in wool. However the Jews were becoming less important to the king as a source of taxes – many were now poor because Henry III had taxed them so much. They were also less important as money lenders. They were being replaced by Italian bankers so the Jews became more vulnerable and faced increasing discrimination and persecution.

- In 1275 a Statute of Jewry in 1275 made it illegal for Jews to lend money. It was designed to encourage them to move into trade or farming. Even so, Edward used a tax on Jewish moneylenders to finance his war with Wales in 1276.
- In 1278 and 1279, most of the Jews in the country were arrested, their houses and property ransacked, and they were accused of money-clipping, as we have already seen (page 30). Nearly 300 were executed as part of the re-coinage process, although only three English people were executed.

Hatred of the Jews was increased by unscrupulous rich people, including the Church, who bought debt from the Jews, and then demanded full and instant repayment which, of course, the landowners could not do. Their only way out was to hand over their land to pay off the debt, thus losing both land and status. King Edward and his wife Eleanor were both known to have used this tactic to their advantage.

The trigger

In 1289, on his return from Gascony, Edward was deeply in debt (again!) and asked Parliament for a tax. This was granted – around £100,000 – in exchange for a law that expelled the Jews from England. In July 1290, Edward signed a law that required all Jews to have left the country by 1 November 1290. This may have been influenced by the case of Isaac de Pulet, who in June 1290, was accused of the murder of a young Christian boy in Oxford.

Reaction

This statute was, according to some historians, the most popular act of Edward's entire reign. One alleged incident shows how some people felt towards the Jews by this time. A sea captain, who was taking a boatload of expelled Jews to the continent, stopped at the mouth of the River Thames and suggested, as it was low tide, his passengers join him for a walk on a nearby sandbank. The captain promptly returned to his ship and sailed away, leaving his Jewish passengers to drown as the tide came in. Rather than being horrified this was widely reported as a rather clever thing to do and a just punishment for those held responsible for the death of Christ.

THINK

3 List all the reasons Jews faced persecution in Edward's England.
4 Which do you think was the most important reason for their expulsion: religion, politics or trade? Explain your answer.
5 What does the fate of the Jews add to our understanding of:
   a) Edward I
   b) England in the 1280s and 1290s?

FOCUS TASK

Winners and losers in Edward's England. Part 2

You have been compiling lists of people (individuals or groups) who either gained or lost from the social changes taking place in the reign of Edward I. Use your notes to write an answer to this question:

'Life was great for people living in Edward I's England'. How far do you agree with this statement?

TOPIC SUMMARY

Trade, towns and villages
- England was fast becoming a cash economy, after 30 years of good harvests.
- Village life was changing, too, as shown by the life of Hugh Cok.
- Towns and trade were increasingly important.
- Wool accounted for perhaps half the wealth of the country.
- Edward was often short of money and, when Parliament was reluctant to vote him a tax, he would borrow money.
- In 1290 the Jews were expelled from England. This action made Edward very popular.
- In 1294 many people opposed Edward's higher export tax on wool.

Clerics

Priests

Around 33,000

Men who were authorised to perform the sacraments of the Church. They were meant to be celibate (unmarried) and reasonably well educated. Good priests might be promoted to be a bishop or even an archbishop.

Monks and nuns

Around 15,000

Men and women who devote their life to God through prayer and poverty and service. Usually live in a monastery or nunnery set up in out-of-the-way places.

Friars

Around 5,000

A new type of monk appeared in the thirteenth century. Friars take a vow of poverty, living on charity from others. They travelled from place to place, and were renowned for their excellent preaching.

FOCUS TASK

What most influenced education and learning during this period?
Part 1

As you work through this topic, make notes to explain how the following influenced people's education and learning.

- Parish priests
- Religious buildings
- Monks and monasteries
- Pilgrimages
- Friars
- Universities

2.2 Education and learning

FOCUS

In the typical medieval village or town there would be no school. Instead education was controlled by the church. Everyone in England belonged to the Catholic Church and attended church every Sunday where they the priest taught them how to live a good life, what to think and how to behave. This gave the parish priests, and the church leaders who supervised them, great power over ordinary people. In this topic you will investigate the role of the church in education and learning and how it was changing in this period.

The presence of the Church

Source 1 shows the front wall of Exeter Cathedral. It dominated the medieval town. It was designed to impress people with its high towers and large windows. The wall is filled with sculptures of angels, and Bible characters including Jesus and Mary and God. At this time many village churches were also being rebuilt in stone. They would not be as grand as Exeter Cathedral but even so the church was often the only stone building in a village and was certainly designed to be the most impressive.

The village church was a place of prayer but was also used for council meetings, inquests or court hearings. The churchyard was often used for markets and fairs.

Just as important as the church buildings were the people – priests, monks, nuns and friars – who worked in them. Together they are known as CLERICS and their roles are explained in the Factfile.

The only way to get an education was to join the church and the parish priest would usually be the most LITERATE and educated person in a village. They might have run a small school teaching only boys Latin, reading and writing. As well as leading church services clerics also provided hospitals for the sick, and hospitality for travelers. The clerics were ever-present in people's everyday lives.

The Church also controlled the only universities in England (Oxford and Cambridge). They owned 20 per cent of all land in England – through which they got very rich. They had their own system of law courts. And they helped the king run the country.

SOURCE 1

Exeter Cathedral, rebuilt in the thirteenth century, in the Decorated style.

The teachings of the Church

At this time ordinary people could not read and the church services were in Latin, which was a language few people understood. So the main ways people were taught what to think and how to behave were through paintings and through sermons.

The walls of most churches would be painted with scenes from the life of Christ, stories from the Bible, or 'DOOM' PAINTINGS. Source 3 is one of the most spectacular that survives to the present day. These paintings taught people how to live a good Christian life so they could get to Heaven.

In 1281, Lambeth Council (so called because Lambeth Palace was the official residence of the Archbishop of Canterbury, the leader of the Church of England) decreed that four times each year every priest should preach, in English, about the fundamental teachings of the Church:

- the Creed – which summarised Christian beliefs about God and Jesus
- the Ten Commandments – for example: 'Thou shalt not kill'; 'Thou shalt not commit ADULTERY', 'Thou shalt not steal'
- the Seven Virtues (good behaviour to cultivate such as kindness, chastity, patience) and the Seven Vices or Seven Deadly Sins (bad behaviour or attitudes to avoid such as pride, gluttony, lust).
- the Seven Works of Mercy (for example to feed the hungry; shelter the homeless, visit the sick, bury the dead.
- and the Seven Sacraments (for example Baptism, Holy Communion, Marriage) through which people got closer to God.

Pilgrimage

With people so aware of the threat of Hell and the promise of Heaven they were always looking for ways to improve their chances of going to Heaven and to reduce the time they spent in Purgatory, the place where your soul awaited judgment after death. The Church offered various routes.

One of the most popular was to go on a pilgrimage. The main places of pilgrimage were the Holy Land (modern day Israel/Palestine), Rome, or the tomb of St James the Apostle at Santiago de Compostela in northern Spain. If you couldn't manage those distances then you could travel to:

- Canterbury, to the tomb of Thomas Becket;
- Glastonbury, where Joseph of Arimathea was supposed to have buried the Holy Grail and where King Arthur was allegedly buried; or to
- Walsingham in Norfolk. Walsingham was particularly special to King Edward, who visited there eleven times to worship at the shrine to the Virgin Mary, the mother of Jesus.

Thousands of people made these pilgrimages, many coming from overseas. When they arrived they prayed but they might also give ALMS, buy food or pilgrim badges (see Source 5) to show they had made the journey. Pilgrims could make a church very wealthy indeed.

SOURCE 2

Extract from the *Handlyng Synne*, by Robert Mannyng, 1303, a poem that was designed to teach less educated priests the basic teachings of the church. and its translation.

The third sin is Envy that is full of evil.

Holy Scripture bears clear witness that it [Envy] comes entirely from the Devil.

The man that is full of envy is always sorrowful: we see with our eye that the good that he seeks after does utter harm to him, and it is all the enticement of the Devil.

Be aware now, therefore, from the start: If you were ever pleased by an unfortunate thing happening to any man, that arose from great envy.

THINK

Study Source 2.

1 What does Source 2 tell us about the way the Church educated priests?

Study Source 3.

2 The picture is showing bad people being punished for evil deeds and good people rewarded for good deeds. See if you can work out sins or virtues are depicted. You can find some answers on page 00.

3 What lesson do you think the viewer was supposed to learn from this painting?

SOURCE 3

A mural in Chaldon church, Surrey showing the Ladder of Souls with the Seven Deadly Sins. This was painted around 1200. Souls in Purgatory are being judged as to whether they go to Heaven or Hell, based on their actions on Earth.

THINK

Study Source 5.

1 Why do you think pilgrims bought badges?
2 What effect do you think making a pilgrimage would have on the people who undertook them?

SOURCE 4

A pilgrim, from an illuminated medieval manuscript.

SOURCE 5

Walsingham pilgrim's badge.

THINK

3 What does the rapid growth of religious houses tell us about the influence and power of the Church?
4 How significant do you think it was that the friars preached their sermons in English?

SOURCE 6

From an illuminated manuscript – a monk at work in the scriptorium (a monastery room where manuscripts were copied).

The growth of religious houses

Throughout the thirteenth century there was a huge growth in the number of monasteries, nunneries, abbeys, and even HERMITAGES.

Monasteries were renowned as places of learning. The Abbot of Durham at this time had a library of over 500 books which had all been copied by hand. The art of making illuminated manuscripts (see Source 6) was practised in most monasteries. Many of the illustrations in this book are taken from such manuscripts, copied out by hand and decorated by monks.

Some monasteries made the own CHRONICLES, the history books of their time, which recorded events year by year. We have already seen the response of the Chronicle of Dunstable Priory to the death of Laurence of Ludlow (see page 30). Peter of Langtoft, who died around 1305, spent most of his life in Bridlington Priory where he wrote a history of England, from the (fictional) founding of the country by Brutus, to the death of Edward I.

Monasteries also served as hospitals for the sick. The most common form of treatment was to pray and ask God's forgiveness for whatever sins had made you ill. However, some monks also became very skilled, both in herbal remedies and sometimes surgery.

The impact of the friars

The biggest shake-up in the Church at this time was the arrival of the friars, who were predominantly from the Orders of the Dominicans and the Franciscans. They rebelled against the increasing wealth of the Church. They took a vow of poverty, and depended on the charity of others to survive. They travelled the country, seeking out audiences wherever they went. They were famous for preaching lively sermons in public places. Donations came flooding in, helping to establish a number of friaries across the country. Their preaching in English made Christianity more accessible and helped to reinvigorate the Church. They are said to have invented Christmas carols, putting Christian stories to popular tunes of the day.

Changing universities

The Franciscans were not only famous for their preaching. They also placed great emphasis on study and learning which had a great impact on the development of England's universities.

At this time England had two established universities: Oxford, set up in the eleventh century, and Cambridge, set up in 1209. By the time of Edward I both universities had an excellent reputation, rivalling Paris. There were over 3,000 students at Oxford in the 1290s.

When the Franciscans first came to England they based themselves in Oxford. They set up a training college there in 1290 then further colleges in Durham in the same year for clerics from the north of the country, and in Gloucester in 1291 for clerics from the south.

Virtually all of the teachers and students were clerics and teaching was by lecture and debate. As a student you had to find, and pay for, your own teacher. Books were expensive and scarce. Students were expected to study grammar, RHETORIC, LOGIC, arithmetic, geometry, astronomy and music. But as the century progressed, the curriculum began to widen. The Franciscans were responsible for adding science and medicine.

They were helped by the fact that the Crusades had opened up access to the ancient texts which had been preserved and translated by Arabic scholars. These were copied and gradually became more available through the Christian world through the monasteries and universities. The impact of the Crusades was much more than just fighting!

Roger Bacon: scientist extraordinaire

Roger Bacon was a Franciscan friar who studied at Oxford and in Paris, as well as teaching in both universities. He was born in 1214, but very little is known of his early life. During his time at Oxford he developed a reputation as a 'seeker of the truth' using what was then known as the EMPIRICAL method – nowadays we would call it scientific investigation.

At the request of Pope Clement IV, he compiled his *Opus Maius*, which was an encyclopaedia of all known science, including his own work on light and lenses (see Source 7). Roger Bacon is said to have invented reading glasses! Like many scientists at the time, he was also interested in alchemy – trying to turn common metals such as lead into gold.

Bacon was no respecter of reputations. Having begun his scientific work based on Aristotle's teachings, he quickly discovered a number of errors. He came up with the theory of four sources of error that prevented progress in science. These were:

1 Reliance on faulty authority.
2 Reliance on popular opinion.
3 Reliance on personal bias.
4 Reliance on rational argument.

All these things, Bacon argued, prevented the discovery of the truth. Needless to say, many of his ideas were very unpopular and it seems at one stage he was thrown out of the Franciscans and put in prison for his ideas. He died in Oxford around 1292, but no one is exactly sure when.

SOURCE 7

Roger Bacon's diagram of light being refracted by a container of water.

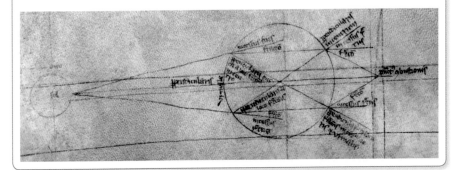

A painting of Duns Scotus by Justus van Gent (1460–80).

Duns Scotus: philosopher and theologian

Duns Scotus, or John Duns, was born around 1265–70 in either Scotland, Ireland or England. No one is sure exactly when or where, although it was probably near Berwick in Scotland. He was a Franciscan who became famous in his own lifetime for the depth of his thinking and the subtlety of his arguments.

He studied at Oxford, and taught in both Oxford and Paris, before finally being asked by the friars to go to Cologne. He became known as the 'Marian Doctor' because of his absolute devotion to Mary, Jesus's mother. He devised the theory of the immaculate conception – a theory that Jesus was born free from sin that only became firm Catholic Church doctrine 600 years later, in 1854.

His ideas were very controversial at the time, and he was often in trouble because of them. It is said he had to leave Paris in a hurry because of the content of one of his lectures. He is reputed to have been the greatest Franciscan scholar of all time. He wrote widely on the nature of the Church, on God's relationship with man, and of God's role in the creation of man.

He died suddenly in Cologne in 1308. On his SARCOPHAGUS in the Franciscan church in Cologne is the legend, 'Scotland brought me forth; England sustained me; France taught me; Cologne holds me'.

FOCUS TASK

Part 2: How important was the Church at this time?

Use your answers to the Focus Task on page 35 to write an answer to the following essay:

'How much influence did the Church have on people?'

KEY WORDS

Make sure you know what these terms mean:
- Cleric
- Priest
- Monk
- Friar
- Pilgrimage
- Chronicle
- Franciscans

TOPIC SUMMARY

Education and learning
- The Church was very important at this time.
- It influenced the way people behaved, as well as the way they prayed.
- There were tensions between friars and other religious groups.
- Education and learning were almost entirely dependent on the Church.
- The Church was sometimes reluctant to embrace new ideas.

THINK

1 What does the inscription on John Duns' sarcophagus tell us about the nature of the Church in the thirteenth century?
2 Why do you think both Roger Bacon and John Duns were often in trouble for their views?
3 From the evidence you have, do you think the Church welcomed new ideas?

2.3 The development of the legal system

FOCUS

You have already seen in Chapter 1 that some historians regard Edward as the 'English Justinian', giving a whole new code of laws to the country. Certainly, when he arrived in England for his coronation in 1274, Edward seemed determined to act. He dismissed most of the sheriffs, set up an investigation into official corruption and started the practice of allowing people to petition Parliament for redress of grievances. Then throughout his reign he issued many statutes designed to improve the legal system. This topic investigates:

● Why Edward I did this
● How successful he was. How fair did Edward's system of justice turn out to be?

FOCUS TASK

How did the legal system develop? Part 1

As you read through this topic note examples of how law and order changed under Edward.

● Highlight in one colour positive examples of improvements made by Edward.
● In another colour highlight negative examples of problems continuing under Edward.

What problems did Edward inherit?

Edward inherited a legal system with lots of problems.

Royal authority was weak

Henry III had been a weak king who found it hard to assert his authority. This allowed the barons, particularly those living far from London, to rule their areas how they wished. They held their own courts, and punished people how they wished. Barons, Lords of the Manor and Sheriffs could bend the rules to their own advantage.

Law enforcement was not very effective

Responsibility for enforcing the law fell to the ordinary people. Every male in each county was part of a TITHING, a group of ten people, who were responsible for ensuring everyone kept the law. If one of their number committed a crime it was the responsibility of the others to hand them over to the courts.

If you were unjustly accused of a crime you could take SANCTUARY in a church, where you were deemed safe for 40 days and for 40 nights. After this time you could make for the nearest port to leave the country. However if your crime was really bad you might be dragged out of the church and punished or even killed by the crowd.

There were sheriffs appointed by the king who were supposed to oversee this system but the sheriff was not a judge or able to find people guilty of a crime. His role was more to implement the King's wishes, and collect taxes for him.

Trials and punishments were inconsistent

There was a system of courts – but because of the collapse of royal authority they could easily be corrupted by local officials. And the system was inefficient. Sometimes people could await trial for ages until a qualified judge visited their area.

Some old-fashioned ways of finding out if someone was guilty were still in use. At the start of Edward's reign you might still come across examples of 'trial by combat' (see Source 1). This involved two sides in a dispute deciding the outcome by fighting – either themselves, or via a champion. Trial by water was also still used in which the accused would be bound and thrown into a river or pond. If they surfaced they were guilty and thus to be punished, and if they sank they were innocent!

SOURCE 1

An early medieval illustration of trial by combat.

THINK

1 What problems can you see with the system of tithings?
2 Do you think this system would lead to justice?
3 What problems can you see with trial by combat and trial by water as a means of finding out whether someone is guilty?

Outlaws

If someone was summoned to trial but ran away instead he could be declared an outlaw which meant they lost all legal rights. They could be killed by anyone or hunted down and handed over for a ransom. Being declared an outlaw was a serious punishment. In Henry's reign there were many outlaws – living in the forests or overseas. People did not trust the legal system enough to agree to stand trial. Some preferred the uncertainty and risk of being an outlaw. However the idea of the noble outlaw (represented by the Robin Hood stories) is largely a myth. Outlaws were actually more likely to be criminal gangs and they could even be in the pay of the local lord who used them terrorise his opponents.

FIGURE 2

A reconstruction drawing of a thirteenth-century court

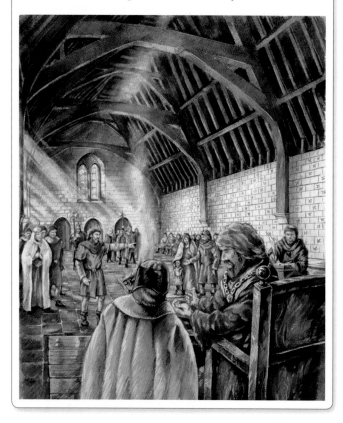

Changes to the courts

Edward made some changes to the courts so that disputes and crimes were dealt with quickly and fairly.

- **Manor or 'leet' courts** – these village courts continued to meet regularly to deal with minor offences or everyday local issues such as blocked roads or ditches, straying animals, disputes over land and so on. Occasionally they also dealt with minor cases of violence, such as the case of William Bunting who was forced to compensate Peter Gill two shillings for beating and ill-treating him.
- **Hundred or borough courts** – these met every two or three weeks and dealt with any cases within their area. A jury of twelve free men would be sworn in to determine the character of the accused and decide if they were guilty. The system of law became known as Common Law. More serious cases were passed to the higher courts.

Edward did not make major changes to the manor courts or the borough courts. His main changes were to the next three levels.

- **Assizes** – the old system (called the general Eyre) was not working well. Accused people could be kept in prison for months or even years, awaiting the arrival of the judges. In 1294 Edward introduced the local Assizes. Judges regularly visited each area so cases could be dealt with promptly.
- **Royal courts** – the King's Bench heard criminal cases and appeals from the lower courts, and the Court of Common Pleas at Westminster dealt with property rights. These were not new but they were used increasingly as the thirteenth century progressed, and many of Edward's laws were geared to reinforcing the role of these courts.
- **Parliament** – this was the highest court in the land. New laws were made here by Statute. Edward introduced the practice of allowing people to petition Parliament for redress of grievances. Any member of the House of Lords had the right to trial by his peers.

Alongside this system of secular courts there were also Church courts.

- **Church courts** had existed since the 1100s. They used canon (or religious) law rather than secular (or king's) law. These courts were mainly used for social matters, such as not attending church on Sunday; disputes over tithe payments; wills; heresy and witchcraft; and cases of sexual misconduct. These courts had a reputation for lesser punishments – sticking strictly to the commandment, 'Thou shalt not kill'.

THINK

1 Which type of court do you think the picture in Figure 2 is supposed to represent? Give your reasons. How convincing is it?
2 Why do you think there were so many different types of court?
3 What benefits and problems might there have been with so many courts?

Statutes

Edward passed more statutes than any other medieval king. You have already come across the Statute of Westminster (see page 17). This made various improvements to law and order including the introduction of the 'Hue and Cry'. Every man in a neighbourhood had to help catch an offender if the hue and cry was raised. The Statute also included measures to control sheriffs and other local officials to ensure good government.

The Statute of Gloucester, 1278

Most of this dealt with land disputes. The process to recover ALIENATED land (called *Novel disseisin* or 'recent dispossession'), was made quicker and easier. Someone who had been unlawfully deprived of their land could now demand compensation for their loss.

Other measures included:

- The process of sending royal justices around the country to hear cases was revived
- The law for accidental murder or killing in self-defence was clarified. Offenders could now apply to the king for a pardon.

Statute of Winchester, 1285

This Statute was passed seven years later. Its PREAMBLE suggests there were still major problems with law and order. It stated: 'Because from day to day robberies, HOMICIDES and arsons are more often committed than they used to be…'

- Each town and borough was to have night watchmen (the number depending on the size of the population) at each gate, which was to be closed at dusk and opened at dawn.
- Brushwood and trees, other than oak trees, were to be cleared 200 feet (70 metres) either side of the King's highway in an attempt to protect travellers from being attacked by OUTLAWS.
- Everyone living in a hundred was to be responsible for each crime and pay damages if the criminal was not apprehended by them.
- Each person in the country, according to their income, was to keep appropriate weapons ready for joining the 'hue and cry' when necessary.

Punishments

Edward introduced harsher punishments to deter criminals from committing crimes. Most notably he introduced the death penalty by hanging as the punishment for stealing goods worth more than 12 pennies. In practice these tougher penalties actually made a jury less willing to convict someone, unless they were truly convinced the accused was guilty, for example if he had been caught in the act. You can see this in Source 3.

Prison

One obvious difference from today is that in medieval England prison was seldom used as a punishment. Prisons were for people awaiting trial. The Clink prison was set up in Southwark, south of the River Thames, by the Bishop of Winchester, but overall few convicted criminals were sent to prison.

Inside prison people without money were treated very poorly, but if you had the means to pay for it you could have food, drink and bedding brought in. It was even possible to rent a comfortable room whilst you were in prison!

FACTFILE

'Benefit of clergy'

If you could claim 'benefit of clergy', you were more likely to escape hanging, even for murder. The test for benefit of clergy was to be able to recite Psalm 51 in Latin; 'O God, have mercy upon me, according to thine heartfelt mercifulness', and it was widely believed that illiterate non-clerics only had to be able to recite the Psalm to escape true justice!

SOURCE 3

Cases submitted to the Eyre of Huntingdon in 1286. From *Edward I*, by Michael Prestwich, p. 283

Men accused of homicide	190
Brought to trial (out of 190)	63
Convicted (out of 63)	17
Men accused of theft	239
Convicted	95

THINK

Study Source 3.

4. What percentage of men accused of homicide were brought to trial?
5. What percentage of men brought to trial for homicide were convicted?
6. What percentage of men accused of theft were convicted?
7. Write two sentences to summarise what these figures suggest about the state of lawlessness and the process of the law in Huntingdon during 1286.

The law in action

Criminal cases (dealing with people who break the law set by king or government)

A man in Bodmin woke up one morning to find one of his horses had been stolen. The next day he saw his horse in the market place in the possession of a man called Robert and raised the 'hue and cry'. Both men were arrested and ordered to appear in court. The lord of the manor, the prior of Bodmin, ordered a court to sit immediately. Robert confessed and was hanged. His fate was sealed by the fact that he was in possession of the horse – there was no discussion of whether or not he actually stole the horse.

Wakelin, the son of Ranulf, killed Matilda Day with a knife. He was caught in the act with a bloodstained knife. He was found guilty and hanged.

Roger de Drayton, the steward of the Earl of Cornwall, was murdered in broad daylight whilst walking to Parliament in London. His assailants sought sanctuary in a church and were thus able to escape abroad.

Civil cases (disputes between individuals)

The Abbot of Westminster was Lord of the Manor of Bourton-on-the-Hill and Todenham in Gloucestershire. He felt that his tenants were not doing their labour services correctly. If the work day fell on a Church Feast Day (and there were over 40 of them in a year), then they didn't work. The Abbot argued that if they missed a day's work for him, they should work on another day as compensation. The tenants disagreed, and refused to work on what they regarded as 'their' days. The Abbot took the tenants to court and won the case. The peasants were each fined for the days they had not fulfilled their obligations, but in a gesture of reconciliation, the Abbot waived the fines. He was upset when the tenants refused to thank him for what they regarded as an unjust victory.

In 1294, the peasants of Penrhoslligwy in Anglesey felt the demands for labour service were unjust and began what became a 40-year campaign to get them reduced. This included, in 1305, a petition to Parliament.

In 1305, the monks of Battle Abbey tried to get the peasants on their estate classified as serfs, thereby reducing their ability to own land. John att Doune, a tenant, brought a successful case in the King's court that led to him being declared a tenant, not a serf.

THINK

Study the six cases summarised on this page.

1 Which examples would you use if you wanted to argue that the legal system was fair and effective in Edward's reign?
2 What examples would you use if you want to argue the opposite?

Explain your choices carefully.

Did Edward succeed?

Despite all Edward's efforts, by the end of his reign, many people thought the legal system in England was still in crisis.

Corruption

Corruption remained a huge problem. In 1294 the Yorkshire Eyre complained that 'justice is completely choked'. Influential men manipulated legal proceedings. Juries were reluctant to find powerful people guilty. Sometimes cases were interrupted by powerful patrons of the accused entering the court and drawing a sword to intimidate the judge. In 1305, Ranull de Friskeney, from Lincolnshire, a royal justice, was convicted of influencing pleas and protecting his friends. He even employed some men he had convicted of violent behaviour to intimidate opponents. A poor woman summoned to appear before the sheriff's clerk at Newcastle gaol went into hiding because the clerk had threatened to rape her and pull out all her teeth once she was in his power.

Part of the problem was that judges were poorly paid, which meant they were susceptible to bribery and corruption.

By the end of Edward's reign it seemed that the problems were actually getting worse. Economic hardship, brought about by Edward's wars and a run of poor harvests, meant that many more people turned to crime as the only option. The number of outlaws increased. Outlaws seemed to be running some parts of the country.

Edward's response

Edward introduced two new processes to deal with what was perceived as a desperate situation.

Twice a year or more if needed judges attended sessions called 'Oyer and Terminer' (which means 'hear and decide'). They had full jurisdiction to empty the goals (ie try anyone awaiting trial), deal with both civil and criminal cases, and deal with them quickly.

In 1305 the Ordinance of Trailbaston (named after a short cudgel used by outlaws) was introduced to deliver swift justice where outlaws seemed to be running the country.

Edward had set out to make the law more efficient, to right wrongs, correct abuses and errors, but by the end of his reign crime levels were worryingly high.

THINK

3 What does the author of this popular song (Source 4) think about judges and justice?
4 What situation is being described in Source 5?

SOURCE 4

From the 'Song on the Venality of Judges', written down at the beginning of the fourteenth century.

Blessed are they who hunger and thirst, and do justice and hate and avoid the wickedness of injustice; they judge what is just, and do not fall off from the right for the sake of the rich.

But now the age deceives many, and draws them into danger, for love of the world, that they may lick up honours.

The cause of this is money, to which almost every court has now wedded itself there are judges, whom bribes seduce; they pay toll to the devil, and they serve him alone for the law of nature commands, that a judge in giving judgment should not accept either prayer or money;

what therefore, O good Jesus, will be done with the judges, who for prayers or gifts leave from what is just?

SOURCE 5

Extracts from a poem, supposedly written in 1306 by an outlaw.

Ill-disposed people, from whom God keeps his pity,

out of their lying mouths have indicted me

of wicked robberies and other crimes,

so that I do not dare visit my friends.

Forty shillings they take for my ransom,

and the sheriff turns up for his bribe

for not putting me in a deep dungeon.

Now, lords, consider, is this fair?

KEY WORDS

Be sure you learn what these words mean and are able to use them confidently in your own writing. See glossary on page 76 for definitions.

- Statute
- Petition
- Sheriff
- Tithing
- Hue and cry
- Sanctuary
- Manor court
- Borough court
- Royal court
- Assizes
- Church court
- Benefit of clergy
- Outlaw
- Bribery

FOCUS TASK

How did the legal system develop? Part 2

Now that you have created your notes, write an answer to the following question:

Write an account of how the legal system developed under Edward I.

In your conclusion consider whether you think Edward improved the situation in England.

TOPIC SUMMARY

The development of the legal system
- Henry III had lost royal authority and Edward was determined to re-establish it.
- Edward attempted to make justice speedier and fairer for all by responding to the perceived problems and complaints.
- He passed many new Statues to deal with worsening situations.
- He changed the court system.
- Corrupt officials often undermined his attempts to make the law fairer.
- owards the end of his reign, wars and poor harvests led to an increase in violence and disorder in the country.

REVIEW OF CHAPTER 2

Life in medieval England

REVIEW TASK

What kind of king was Edward I?

Look back at the introduction to this book, and especially the answer you wrote to the question, 'What kind of king do you think Edward was?' You are now going to review that answer in the light of the work you have completed in Chapter 2.

Part 1

Here is our list of what people expected of a medieval king:

- To defend the country
- To produce an heir
- To keep the law
- To protect the Church
- To ensure people can go about their daily lives in safety and freedom
1 Which of these aspects of kingship are dealt with in Chapter 2?
2 How well do you think Edward has dealt with these aspects of kingship?

Part 2

Draw a 'living graph' like the one below. Place each event above or below the line, depending on whether this shows Edward acting in his own self-interest, or in the interests of 'good government' and the people. The higher or lower you place an event, the stronger it fits that description.

It is possible that an action is in **both** Edward's and the people's interest. If so it should appear twice - both above and below the line. But **how far above** and **how far below** will show how you think the balance falls between Edward's interests and the people's interests.

For example, 'Edward issued new coins in 1279' might be in the interests of the people; the new coins were of different values and removed the need to clip silver pennies to make halfpennies so the event could be placed below the line. However, the re-coinage made a profit of £25,000 for Edward, which worked in his own interest, so the event could appear above the line. Personally, I would place the re-coinage below the line as I believe it was designed to improve trade, and Edward's profit was incidental.

There is no one correct answer to any of these issues! You just have to be sure that you have evidence to support your judgement. So for each item you place add a short explanation for your placing – supporting it with evidence from the chapter.

Acting in Edward's best interests

1275   1280   1285   1290   1295   1300   1305

Acting in the people's best interests

1300 40,000 sacks of wool exported

1293 Edward buys the town of Kingston upon Hull from monks

1286 Lincoln paves its main streets

1279 Re-coinage

1274 Customs duty of 7s 6d imposed on exports of wool

1275 Statute of Jewry prohibits money lending

1281 Lambeth Council decree on preaching

1290 Jews expelled from England

1279 Edward issues new coins

1292 Death of Roger Bacon

1308 Death of John Duns

1294 Oyer and Terminer introduced

1294 Local assizes replace general Eyre

1278 Statute of Gloucester

1305 Ordinance of Trailbaston

1285 Statute of Winchester

1289 Funeral of Henry Poche

1305 Tenants of Penrhosliugwy present a petition to Parliament over their rights

Practice Questions

Here is another opportunity to use practice questions to review your learning. In your exam you will be set four questions on the British depth study.

Question 1 will be 'an interpretation question'. You will need to use your knowledge to explain how convincing an interpretation is. The interpretation could be written or visual. For example:

1. How convincing is Figure 3 (page 9) in helping us understand life in a medieval town? (8 marks)

For this question you should aim to describe what you can see and then use detailed knowledge to support and contradict what the source tells you about medieval town life. Try to find at least three points on either side – convincing and not convincing.

Use the questions below to help you get started.
- can you find examples of things that would make living in towns unhealthy, such as dumping waste in the river?
- can you find examples of accidents or crime?
- can you find any examples of the town council attempting to make conditions better, as suggested on page 28?
- can you find examples of trade linking village and town, as the example of Hugh Cok (page 26) suggests?
- are you convinced by the artist and his modern picture of medieval town life? Why?

Question 2 will ask you to 'explain' something – for example some development or change in the period. It is testing your knowledge and understanding. For example:

2. Explain what was important about the economic changes that took place in Edward's England. (8 marks)

There are many things you could cover but you should focus on those that show the importance of the statutes not the incidental details.

1 Which of the following do you think you should spend most time on?
- cash economy and increase in rented land
- increased imports and exports
- growth of towns
- gave rich people more power over the king
2 Look back at Topic 2.1 to see how you could expand on your chosen point.

Question 3 asks you to write an account. This is a 'narrative' question, testing your knowledge and understanding and analysis of historical events. For example:

3. Write an account of the role of the Church in Edward's England. (8 marks)

For this question you should aim to cover a range of events and developments with enough detail to show you understand the different aspects of the Church and how they helped or harmed Edward's government. You could include:
- influencing the way people thought and behaved
- the part the Church played in running the country
- the role of monasteries and hospitals and advances in medicine
- the arrival of the Friars and their impact

Look back at Topic 2.2 and write a paragraph on at least one of these points. make sure you connect it back to the focus of the question which is about the role of the church.

Question 4 will be on the historic environment. You will be given a statement about the period and you will be asked to reach a judgement on how far a historical site you have studied supports the statement. You should be balanced and analytical but the key will be to make a judgement about how far the statement is true and to write a coherent essay to back up your judgement.

We don't know which site you will study as it changes every year but you can practice with any site. One of the sites that has been mentioned in this chapter is Stokesay Castle (see page 31).

Read the information on pages 31–3 about the castle and its owner Laurence of Ludlow and use it plan our an answer to one or two of these questions.
- what does the story of Laurence of Ludlow tell us about the importance of the wool trade in Edward's time?
- what does the style of the house tell us about how safe the country was at this time?
- what does it tell us about the importance of wool merchants to Edward?
- is the fact that the house has been changed very little since the thirteenth century important?

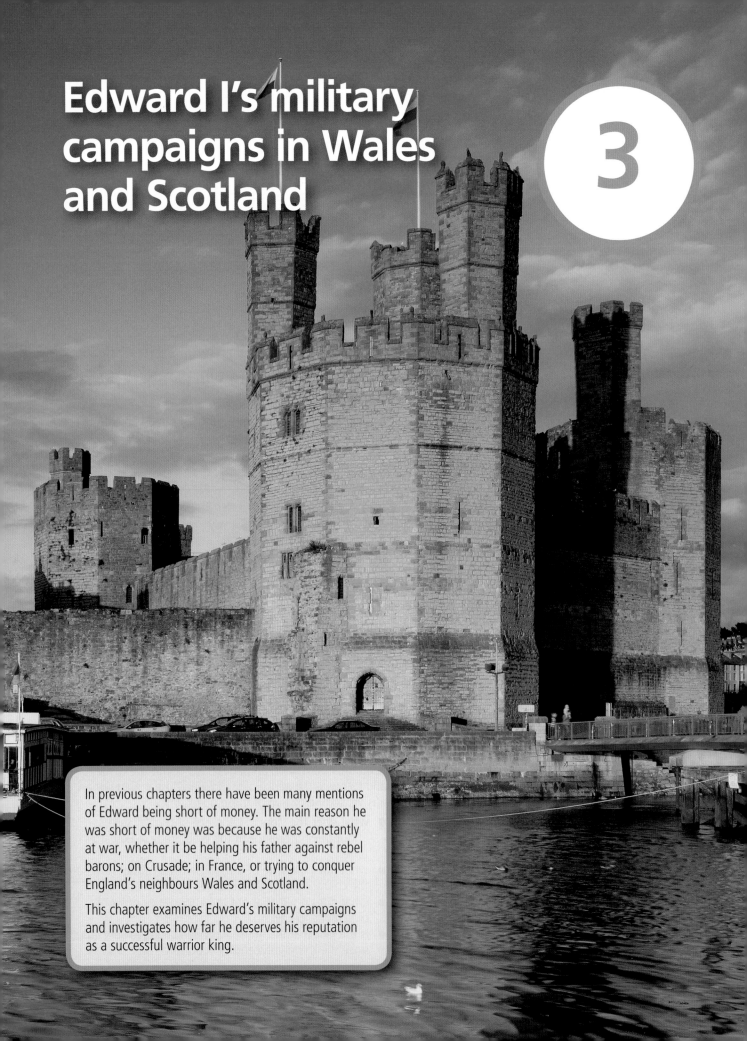

Edward I's military campaigns in Wales and Scotland

3

In previous chapters there have been many mentions of Edward being short of money. The main reason he was short of money was because he was constantly at war, whether it be helping his father against rebel barons; on Crusade; in France, or trying to conquer England's neighbours Wales and Scotland.

This chapter examines Edward's military campaigns and investigates how far he deserves his reputation as a successful warrior king.

Chivalry: King Arthur and the Round Table

On 19 April 1278, Edward and his wife Eleanor were in Glastonbury, in Somerset. They were there to oversee the transfer of the bones of King Arthur and his Queen, Guinevere, to a new tomb, in the NAVE of Glastonbury Abbey, just below the High Altar. King Arthur was the legendary English king who led the fight against Saxon invaders in the fifth and sixth centuries, after the collapse of Roman control.

The monks of Glastonbury had 'discovered' the remains of Arthur and his wife in 1199, just after a disastrous fire had destroyed much of the Abbey. Pilgrims had flocked to the grave of the legendary king, and Glastonbury became a major place of pilgrimage, making the Abbey very rich in the process! Now Edward was joining in the celebrations.

Arthur may not even have existed – there is no clear agreement between historians on the issue. However there is no doubting the power of the legend. The stories of King Arthur and his chivalrous Knights of the Round Table figure strongly in many medieval romances. Geoffrey of Monmouth wrote about Arthur in his book in the 1130s, and by the time of Edward I the stories were widely known and retold.

Edward himself was fascinated by King Arthur. According to legend, King Arthur was given a round table as a wedding gift so that all his leading knights could sit *equally* at his table. The story is that Edward had a similar table made for himself in 1290 and the table now hangs in the Great Hall in Winchester Castle (see Source 1).

The significance of this story is that King Arthur and his knights were seen as examples of perfect knightly behaviour: righting wrongs, protecting damsels in distress, slaying dragons and evil knights, and were thus seen as a role model for medieval knights to copy. Edward drew inspiration from Arthur. He used the story of Arthur to justify his conquest of Wales and modelled his castles on those described in the legends.

SOURCE 1

The Round Table that hangs in the Great Hall of Winchester Castle. It has been dated to the 13th or early 14th century, supporting the claim that it was commissioned by Edward I.

THINK

1   Conduct your own research to find out more about the story of King Arthur. What messages does the story deliver about knightly behaviour?

2   Why were the monks of Glastonbury so keen to have a tomb for Arthur?

3   What message was Edward sending out by being in Glastonbury in April 1278?

3.1 Medieval warfare: Tactics and technology

FOCUS

Edward was often at war. For his various campaigns Edward I put together the largest armies ever seen in medieval England. He did not depend as earlier kings had done on feudal services. Instead he wanted paid soldiers that he could depend on. This topic explores the make-up of his army and the tactics and technology he used.

FOCUS TASK

Which part of Edward's army was the most important? Part 1

For each part of the medieval army that you come across in this topic, make notes in your own copy of the table below, about its make-up, weapons and their use in battle.

Part of army	Equipment	Function
Cavalry		
Infantry		

THINK

Study Source 2.
1. How important were the cavalry in a medieval army?
2. What do the infantry wear?
3. Compare the infantry in Source 1 with the cavalry in Source 1. How are they similar? How are they different?

The make-up of a medieval army

The Statute of Winchester in 1285 stated that each man in the country should have weapons appropriate to his station, and to use them as part of the 'hue and cry' to catch criminals, or in times of war. For ordinary people, this might include a white tunic, knives or swords, bows or spears, perhaps even a crossbow. For knights, this would include a war horse, armour of some kind and a sword or lance.

Cavalry

These were the shock-troops of a medieval army – well armed and highly trained. Their job was to charge and destroy the infantry, thus breaking the opposing forces. They were numbered in hundreds, rather than thousands. At the Battle of Falkirk, for example, Edward had 800 mounted cavalry from his household with him.

Horse

The horse was probably the most expensive part of a knight's equipment; Edward once paid £66 for a special war horse (or destrier), although the usual cost might be £10, which was a fortune for many people.

Armour

Armour would depend on wealth. Most knights wore chain mail, but some could only afford hardened leather. Protection was increased by adding extra layers. A HELM (a helmet) was essential, but might be open or closed. Weapons were usually a lance and sword, although some preferred a MACE or an axe.

Shield

Each would carry a wooden shield displaying his arms to identify him. Identification might heighten your fame from brave deeds, or ignominy if you ran away; or might save your life – an opponent might identify you and not kill you, holding you for ransom instead.

Commanders had to use their cavalry with care as they were expensive and very difficult to replace.

Knights prepared for battle through tournaments (see page 52).

SOURCE 1

A. cavalry B. infantry fighting. From the *Holkham Bible*, circa 1326.

Infantry

Edward called up infantry in their thousands, sometimes 20,000 of them or more, although we have no way of knowing exactly how many turned up, and how many fought. Desertion was common, especially as pay became increasingly unreliable. Often villages were expected to supply a quota; sometimes criminals were pardoned if they agreed to fight; sometimes men joined voluntarily for the pay of 2d a day – this was often the case with Welshmen who seem to have served Edward in large numbers, as did many Irishmen:

The infantry were usually split into archers and foot soldiers.

- The **archers** were expected to stop a cavalry charge with arrows and to kill as many of the opposing infantry as possible, to weaken their defensive position.
- The **foot soldiers**, armed with anything from farm implements to swords and shields, would advance on the enemy in a tight mass and force them from the field. Of course, infantry were very vulnerable to a cavalry charge and so it was important to try to protect them by a suitable choice of situation, for example, hedges or boggy ground, which would make it difficult for the cavalry to gain momentum. One tactic used to try to protect the infantry from a cavalry charge was long wooden spikes driven into the ground at an angle. If they were stout enough they could stop the cavalry breaking through. Another technique developed by the Scots was for the infantry to form circles, or schiltroms (see Figure 2). As long as the circles remained tightly packed, then the cavalry would be held at bay. Unfortunately any infantry outside the circle were easy prey for the cavalry.

THINK

1 How important were the infantry?
2 Which part of it was most important?
3 Why?

Specialists

Each army needed specialists too.

Edward called up thousands of **woodcutters**, for instance, on his Welsh campaigns, to chop down trees and make roads for his army.

He also needed **carpenters** (who were paid double that of infantrymen), **smiths, engineers and miners**. In 1303, Edward ordered a wooden bridge to be built in King's Lynn, in portions, and brought up to Scotland by sea. It was to be assembled and used to cross the Firth of Forth, thus allowing Edward's army into northern Scotland without having to use Stirling Bridge. In the end the bridge was not needed, but it shows the careful planning and detail Edward entered into in his preparations for war.

Perhaps the most important specialists were the **supply people**. It is extremely difficult to feed and supply an army of perhaps 20,000 without careful planning and support. Where possible, supplies were brought by river or sea, which was much cheaper than by land. Nevertheless, huge quantities of wheat for bread, ale and wine to drink, and oats for the horses were required to keep a medieval army on the move. He even employed 3,000 people to harvest grain when he captured Anglesey in 1277 and thus feed his army. Edward became quite skilled at this, but still found it difficult to feed and supply his armies – when supplies were lowest desertions were highest!

Sieges could be a long and costly business. At Caerlaverock, for example, a force of 60 Scots held up the whole English army for several weeks. The feature film *Braveheart*, released in 1995, is a largely fictional account of the life of William Wallace and his role in the Scottish Wars with Edward. But it does have some excellent action sequences that you can watch to get a good idea of what it might actually have been like to participate in battle at this time.

FIGURE 2

A modern illustration of English knights attacking a Scottish schiltrom.

FIGURE 3

A modern artist's impression of laying siege to a medieval castle

Siege warfare

All the information on page 51 applies to battles in open warfare. In fact, many medieval battles were sieges. There was a very clear etiquette involved in siege WARFARE. The attacking army would approach the castle or town and demand surrender, giving a time (up to 40 days in some cases) in which to do so. This was to give those in charge the chance to seek instructions from their lord or king. Meanwhile all routes in and out of the town or castle would be blocked off by the attackers, hoping to starve out the defenders. The clear aim was to capture the town or castle without fighting a long and costly battle.

Once the specified time was up then, as Figure 3 shows, there were several ways to try to break into a castle. The most dangerous was by direct assault using ladders. As garrisons were often small – Caerlaverock Castle, for instance, was defended by just 60 men – if you spread your assault around the site you might break in. More likely you could try to break down the walls using SIEGE ENGINES or undermining to collapse a wall or tower. When King John laid siege to Rochester Castle in 1215, he filled the excavated tunnel with the carcasses of 40 fat pigs and by burning these, wooden supports in the tunnel were burned which collapsed the tunnel and tower above.

Specialist weapons were used to besiege castles. Battering rams were used to try to force entry via the main gate; trebuchets, or giant catapults were used by Edward at the siege of Caerlaverock in 1300, and a huge siege-tower was built and used at Bothwell in 1301. During the siege of Stirling Castle, in 1304, we find Edward having sulphur and saltpetre (components of gunpowder) brought to the siege from England, and hurled inside the castle to try to burn down the buildings inside.

At Stirling Castle, there were thirteen siege engines used. Edward built his largest engine yet – called Warwolf. It took 50 workers over three months to build it, and, when dismantled, it needed 30 wagons to move it around. It hurled a missile weighing 300 pounds. When they saw the size of it, the castle defenders wanted to surrender, but Edward refused their offer – he wanted to see his new siege engine at work! One missile from it brought down part of the castle wall. Immediately the castle surrendered.

SOURCE 4

Caerlaverock Castle from the air as it is today.

SOURCE 5

Description of the Siege of Caerlaverock, c. 1300, written by a member of Edward's army.

Caerlaverock was so strong a castle that it feared no siege before the King came there, for it would never have had to surrender, provided that it was well supplied, when the need arose, with men, engines and provisions ... So stoutly was the gate of the castle assailed by him, that never did smith with his hammer strike his iron as he and his did there. Notwithstanding, there were showered upon them such huge stones, quarrels, [arrows from crossbows] and arrows, that with wounds and bruises they were so hurt and exhausted, that it was with very great difficulty they were able to retire.

THINK

1 What impression of Caerlaverock Castle do you get from the writer of Source 5?
2 Taken together, do Sources 4 and 5 suggest Caerlaverock was difficult to break into?

Tournaments

Tournaments were great events in Edward's time. Knights were known to travel hundreds of miles to take part. At this time, they were usually mock battles, between two sides, often over an area several miles wide, rather than the ritualised jousting of later times. Injuries and deaths were common, but so was the opportunity to find fame and fortune; especially in front of the ladies. It was where a knight learned the art of war.

English contests became so savage that the Church eventually forbade the Christian burial of those killed in tournaments. 'Those who fall in TOURNEYS will go to hell,' scolded one monk. Clearly, in many cases, things were getting out of hand! In 1292, the Statute of Arms for Tournaments was ordained, which provided new laws for tournaments. It stated that no pointed weapons should be used, they should be blunted; and that tournaments had to be properly organised and only authorised combatants were allowed to carry arms. After this, tournaments became more regulated and less dangerous for participants, but no less glamorous for knights.

THINK

Study Source 6.

3 Can you distinguish two different sides in the battle?
4 Does the fighting seem fair and well regulated?
5 How do tournaments tie in with the idea of CHIVALRY?
6 How do tournaments prepare knights for war?

FOCUS TASK

Which part of Edward's army was the most important? Part 2

1 Using the information you have collected throughout this topic, you now need to decide which part of the army was most important, and why. It might help you to decide if you place each part of the army along a line like this:

Most important	Least important

2 Discuss your findings in small groups. Do other people in your group agree with your decision?
3 Did the importance of some parts of the army increase during Edward's reign, or decrease?

TOPIC SUMMARY

Medieval warfare, tactics and technology

● The Statute of Winchester 1285, ensured that each man was equipped to fight as and when necessary, according to his station in life.
● Knights were the shock troops of a medieval army; their use was designed to disperse the opposing army.
● Infantry were divided into bowmen and spearmen; each was used differently in battle.
● Supplying an army in the field effectively was the key to success.

SOURCE 6

A Tournament from the *Codex Manesse*, a German medieval songbook, depicting the mêlée, produced around 1305–10.

3.2 The invasion and colonisation of Wales

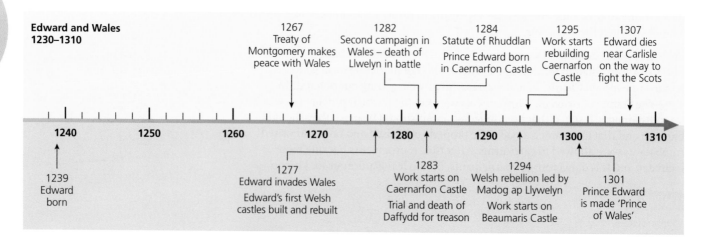

**Edward and Wales
1230–1310**

1240 1250 1260 1270 1280 1290 1300 1310

1267
Treaty of Montgomery makes peace with Wales

1282
Second campaign in Wales – death of Llwelyn in battle

1284
Statute of Rhuddlan
Prince Edward born in Caernarfon Castle

1295
Work starts rebuilding Caernarfon Castle

1307
Edward dies near Carlisle on the way to fight the Scots

1239
Edward born

1277
Edward invades Wales
Edward's first Welsh castles built and rebuilt

1283
Work starts on Caernarfon Castle
Trial and death of Daffydd for treason

1294
Welsh rebellion led by Madog ap Llywelyn
Work starts on Beaumaris Castle

1301
Prince Edward is made 'Prince of Wales'

FOCUS

Edward claimed overlordship of Wales, and expected the Welsh leader Llywelyn ap Gruffudd to acknowledge this. Llywelyn repeatedly refused to do so and this led to a series of rather one-sided wars. Edward spent thousands of pounds defeating the Welsh, and turning Wales into part of England. He built a string of castles and new towns and changed Welsh law to English law, fundamentally changing Wales in the process. This topic will explore the process and ask how Edward was able to achieve this.

Background

In 1264, Llywelyn had been sided with Simon de Montfort against Henry III, and was rewarded with the title 'Prince of Wales'. Henry III had no choice but to accept the situation when he was restored as King, and Llywelyn paid homage to Henry as his OVERLORD. The Treaty of Montgomery, in 1267, acknowledged that Llewelyn had the right to rule Wales, although this alienated many of the Marcher Lords who had lost lands to Llywelyn during the civil war.

Matters came to a head when Llywelyn refused to attend Edward's coronation in 1274, and then repeatedly refused to swear an oath of allegiance or pay dues to Edward as his overlord. As we know, Edward was very touchy about the question of his traditional rights!

FACTFILE

The Treaty of Montgomery, 1267

- Henry III recognised Llywelyn as Prince of Wales.
- Henry III acknowledged Llywelyn's right to rule over Wales.
- Llywelyn agreed to do homage to Henry III as his overlord and pay the English king 25,000 marks. (1 mark = two-thirds of £1)

FOCUS TASK

Why was Edward able to defeat the Welsh? Part 1

As you work through this topic:

1 Make a list of factors that enabled the English to defeat the Welsh. For each factor you find, make a card with a title and brief bullet points on it, like the one shown below.
2 For each factor, decide if it shows English strength or Welsh weakness. Split the cards into two piles as you work through the topic.

Factor: Edward could get supplies from all of the countries he ruled.
  – a fleet from the Cinque Ports
  – war horses from France
  – food from Ireland

1277: It's war!

Edward gave Llywelyn several opportunities to swear loyalty and, perhaps as importantly from Edward's point of view, to pay the money owed under the Treaty of Montgomery. In November 1276, Parliament decreed that Llywelyn was 'a rebel and a disturber of the peace', so Edward began preparations for war.

FIGURE 1

Wales after the Treaty of Montgomery in 1267 and the position of Edward's castles after 1277.

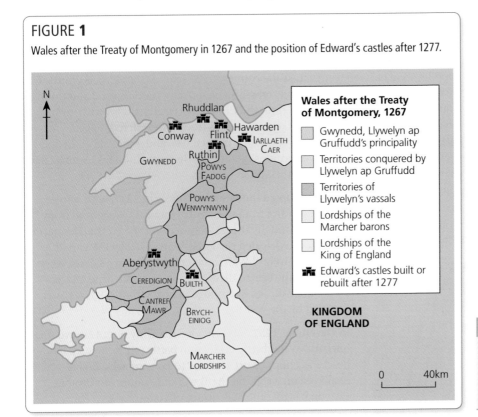

Wales after the Treaty of Montgomery, 1267

- Gwynedd, Llywelyn ap Gruffudd's principality
- Territories conquered by Llywelyn ap Gruffudd
- Territories of Llywelyn's vassals
- Lordships of the Marcher barons
- Lordships of the King of England
- Edward's castles built or rebuilt after 1277

KINGDOM OF ENGLAND

0   40km

THINK

3 Why do you think Edward built his castles where he did?

4 What message is Edward trying to send to the Welsh people with his castles?

Edward's first Welsh campaign

Supplies were ordered from all of Edward's lands, including Ireland and Gascony. He assembled a huge army: 1,000 knights and 15,000 infantry (9,000 of whom were Welsh), along with wood-cutters, smiths and carpenters.

The Marcher Lords invaded from south and mid-Wales, and Edward and his army headed for Chester. From there he advanced to Flint, then Rhuddlan, then Conwy, clearing woodland and creating a road for his army as he went, while a fleet from the CINQUE PORTS isolated Anglesey. Edward sent a force to occupy Anglesey, thus depriving the Welsh of grain, and instead harvesting and using the grain to feed his own army. Llywelyn was increasingly isolated as his VASSALS and other Welsh princes surrendered to Edward or changed sides.

In November, Llywelyn signed the Treaty of Aberconwy, acknowledging Edward as his overlord and surrendering all his recent gains, leaving him solely in charge of Gwynedd. His brother Dafydd ap Gruffydd was given some of Llywelyn's lands as a reward for supporting Edward. Llywelyn was taken to Westminster where he had to do homage in front of Parliament. Edward organised and paid for his wedding to the daughter of Simon de Montfort.

Tensions continue

But this would not be the end of the story. Llywelyn felt put upon by Edward. English officials acted in a high-handed way in Wales. Many, like Edward himself, thought the Welsh uncivilised and inferior. Welsh messengers were arrested without reason, and Marcher Lords killed Welshmen, often without facing trial. Tensions between the English and Welsh started to rise.

Castle building

To consolidate his control and to emphasise English power, Edward built a string of castles designed to hem in Llywelyn. Castles at Builth, Aberystwyth, Flint, Rhuddlan, Ruthin and Hawarden were all either built or rebuilt following the events of 1277 (see Figure 1). Other existing royal castles were strengthened. These castles were expensive to build, and some took 20 years to complete. These castles were to be centres of royal power and administration and courts. English law was introduced for criminal cases, although in Marcher areas, Marcher law would prevail. The castles were a visual reminder to every Welsh person of English presence and power.

1282–83: Revolt and defeat

In Easter week 1282, Dafydd ap Gruffydd attacked and destroyed the still unfinished castle at Hawarden. At the same time, others attacked royal castles across Wales in what was obviously a co-ordinated rebellion. They even attacked the border town of Oswestry. The Welsh had had enough of overbearing English laws and being treated, as they saw it, in an inferior way. Llywelyn knew nothing of the rebellion initially but found he was forced to join in. Edward was outraged. 'My generosity is repaid by rebellion!' he fumed and set about mustering a force to deal with the Welsh.

Supplies were ordered from across the country to be sent to Chester and Worcester. He ordered war horses from France, crossbowmen from Gascony, food and troops from Ireland and Scotland, ships from the Cinque Ports, all paid for with money from the Riccardi, his Italian bankers. As well as troops, he ordered diggers, carpenters, smiths and masons. He ordered timber, oats and grain, ale and wine; everything was stockpiled in enormous quantities. He wanted to make sure he had the supplies to finish off the job this time.

Edward adopted the same strategy as in 1277, with armies attacking Wales from the south, from mid-Wales and from the north. Initially things went well for the Welsh. Their army in the south defeated the English army led by the Earl of Gloucester. In mid-Wales, the English advance slowed when Mortimer, the leader, died. In the north a surprise attack by the English, across a bridge of boats from Anglesey, was defeated by the Welsh.

In December 1282, Llywelyn led his army out of Snowdonia into mid-Wales but was killed in battle (see Source 2). His head was chopped off and sent to Edward, who had it displayed on a spike at the Tower of London. His brother Dafydd became the new Prince of Wales.

The Archbishop of Canterbury had tried to negotiate a settlement, but by now it was too late to compromise. Edward was determined to finish the job. New troops were called up, and Parliament asked to approve a tax.

The King decided on an unprecedented winter campaign. The English armies pressed forward, recapturing all the lost ground. Daffydd asked for peace, but was turned down.

In early March 1283, Edward invaded Gwynedd, the last Welsh stronghold. Slowly but surely, rebels were hunted down and killed. Many made their peace with Edward.

Finally Daffydd was captured. He was put on trial for treason in front of Parliament which was meeting in Shrewsbury. He was found guilty, then hanged, drawn and quartered. Edward took hostages to force each town and village to submit to him as their Lord.

The war had cost Edward £120,000, which was an enormous sum. The tax awarded by Parliament accounted for £50,000, but most of the rest was borrowed and needed to be paid back.

SOURCE 2

The death in battle of Llywelyn. An illustration from a medieval manuscript, *Cotton Nero II*, f.182. Source: © British Library.

The aftermath: The Statute of Rhuddlan, 1284

SOURCE 3

Preamble to the Statute of Rhuddlan, March 1284.

The Divine Providence, which is unerring in its own government, among the gifts of its dispensation, wherewith it hath vouchsafed to distinguish us and our realm of England, hath now of its favour, wholly and entirely transferred under our proper dominion, the land of Wales, with its inhabitants, heretofore subject unto us, in feudal right, all obstacles whatsoever ceasing; and hath annexed and united the same unto the crown of the aforesaid realm, as a member of the same body...

The Statute of Rhuddlan was Edward's attempt to solve the Welsh problem once and for all. Ruled by Edward I, Gwynedd was divided into four English counties: Anglesey, Merionethshire, Caernarvonshire and Flintshire; each to be ruled by a royal official. Sheriffs, coroners and bailiffs would collect taxes and administer justice as in any other English county. Money would be sent to the Exchequer at Westminster. English common law would apply throughout Wales, although the Welsh practice of dividing an estate equally between all the children was retained. Wales in effect became part of England.

More castles

Further castles were built under the supervision of Master James of St George, a master mason from Savoy, whom Edward had met on his way home from his Crusade. They were the latest in military technology and designed to be impregnable. They were to be supplied mostly by sea and thus easily reinforced in times of trouble, but were also designed to show off the wealth and power of the English King. Edward is said to have spent around £80,000 on castle-building in Wales between 1277 and 1304, to ensure there would be no need for further military expeditions.

Many of the new castles had an ADJACENT TOWN, with walls connected to the castle and a port, as in Conway, designed as a safe haven for merchants and others to carry out their business. Merchants and traders from England, France, Ireland and Gascony were encouraged to come to Wales, to help build a cash economy. Cheap rents encouraged settlers, but no Welsh were allowed to live in these new towns.

Some of these castles took over twenty years to complete, and progress was quicker when Edward had money and slower when other problems, like war with France or Scotland, limited his funds. Harlech Castle, for example, took seven and a half years to build at a cost of £9,000 (at a time when a knight's income might be £60 or £100 a year). For most of that time there were 950 workmen employed on site.

These magnificent castles served their purpose and provided safe havens for English officials to carry out the day-to-day business of ruling Wales.

THINK

1 Study Source 3. What does Edward mean by the following phrases?
   a) 'Divine Providence'
   b) 'all obstacles whatsoever ceasing'
   c) 'annexed'
2 Why does Edward insist that Wales be united with the English Crown?
3 By what right does he claim the Welsh Crown?
4 Why did Edward build so many castles if the Welsh threat was destroyed?
5 Why were new towns linked to the castles?
6 'Edward's castles were a complete waste of money.' Do you agree?

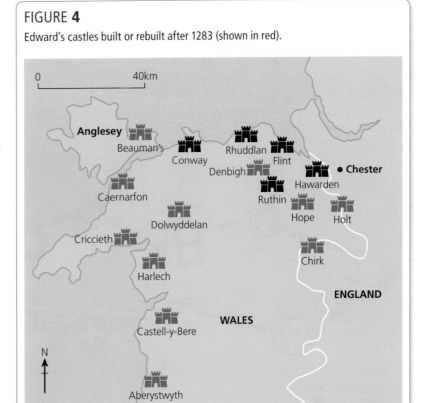

FIGURE 4

Edward's castles built or rebuilt after 1283 (shown in red).

Caernarvon Castle

Caernarvon was conceived as the greatest of Edward's castles, for a variety of reasons. Caernarvon itself was the centre of the Kingdom of Gwynedd, at the crossroads between Anglesey and Snowdonia, and thus building an English castle there made a powerful statement. It was also the site of the Roman town of Segontium, with associations with Magnus Maximus, father of the Emperor Constantine, who ruled the Roman Empire from 306AD to 337AD. Indeed the body of Maximus was said to have been discovered in Caernarvon in 1283 and reburied in the church there, on Edward's specific orders. There were the remains of a Norman motte and bailey castle here too, and the site was incorporated into Edward's castle. Master James of St George was given full rein to build a suitable centre of English power and authority.

Features

The POLYGONAL TOWERS were very different in style and decoration to other Edwardian castles. Few other English castles use polygonal towers. They were based on the walls of Constantinople, both in shape and in the use of multi-coloured layers of stone in their construction. They were built for strength but also to impress. This was a conscious decision by Edward to link his power and authority to the legendary past of Rome and Empire.

Construction

Work started on the site in 1283, when existing houses were demolished to make way for the initial bank and ditch. Soil excavated from the ditch was used to build up the quay beside the River Seiont, where it entered the sea. A timber PALISADE was thrown up all around the site of the castle and new town. The new quay meant supplies could be shipped in from Liverpool, Dublin, Yarmouth, Swansea and even Calais and Boulogne. Stone for the walls came from Anglesey, and lead for the roofs from Bristol. Many of the supplies were brought in from Rhuddlan, including the timber for the palisade that had originally been allocated for the defence of Rhuddlan. Edward's was born here in 1284 so an early priority was timber housing for the royal entourage. By 1285, masons were at work on the town wall. Edward spent £10,000 on Caernarvon Castle between 1283 and 1292. It was meant to be impressive!

Prince of Wales

On 25 April 1284, amidst the building works and part-finished castle of Caernarvon, Edward's son, Edward – the future Edward II – was born. He was the first English prince to be born in Wales. According to some stories, Edward had promised to present the Welsh people with a prince that spoke not a word of English, and this he had done.

FIGURE 6

Plan of Caernarvon Castle, including the dates of the building. Notice that building went on for up to 40 years!

Revolt and destruction

In September 1294, led by Madog ap Llywelyn (a distant relative of Llywelyn), many of the Welsh rose in a new rebellion against Edward. Edward had just levied a tax of one-fifteenth on everyone in Wales to pay for his French war, and the rebels had hoped to attack by the end of September while Edward's troops were in France. Caernarvon, still unfinished, was overrun by the Welsh, sacked and burned to the ground. For six months the Welsh were in control of the castle and the town, and dismantled most of the town walls. Unfortunately for the Welsh, bad weather had prevented Edward's army from sailing, so he was able to turn around his huge army of 35,000 men waiting to embark at Portsmouth, and head for Wales. One part of the army was used to relieve Brecon in the south of the country, while the other part headed for Chester. In a bitter winter campaign, where for a time Edward was besieged without supplies in his new castle of Conwy, the English gradually gained the upper hand and beat the Welsh.

Reconstruction

Once the English had put down the rebellion, Edward started building again at Caernarvon. By 1295, over 200 masons were at work on the site, and Edward spent a further £10,000 at Caernarvon over the following ten years. Work on most of Edward's castles was halted after 1296 when Edward's wars with Scotland began (see page 62), Caernarvon was one of only two sites in the country where building carried on building! The other was Beaumaris Castle, on Anglesey (see page 60).

Subsequent history of Caernarvon Castle

Caernarvon remained the centre of royal authority in Wales until the seventeenth century, although some of the planned works were never finished and no monarch visited Caernarvon until 1911.

- By 1620 many of the buildings were in disrepair, only the Eagle Tower and King's Gate, had roofs!
- During the English Civil War, the castle was garrisoned by Royalists and besieged three times before surrendering in 1646.
- The government paid for some repairs to the structure during the 1870s and the castle was used in 1911 for the INVESTITURE of the future Edward VIII as Prince of Wales. Similarly, the investiture of Prince Charles took place at Caernarvon in 1969.
- In 1986, Caernarvon Castle and the town walls were made a UNESCO World Heritage Site.

THINK

1 Why was Edward's main castle in Wales built at Caernarvon?
2 How did Edward use history to reinforce the role and status of Caernarvon Castle?

Look carefully at the plan of the castle (Figure 6).

3 Why do you think the castle is so long and narrow?
4 In your opinion, was the castle mainly for defence or to display the King's power?
5 In what ways does Speed's map show Edward's success at making Caernarvon a centre of English power and authority?

SOURCE 7

A map of Caernarvon in 1610 by the famous mapmaker John Speed. You can clearly see the strategic importance of the castle from the map, as well as the walls adjoining the castle and encircling the town.

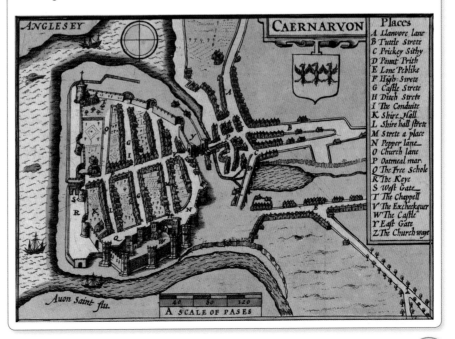

The final acts

Anglesey had been particularly rebellious in 1294 and, to ensure this never happened again, Edward embarked on building another castle, at Beaumaris. Although this was never finished, it is regarded as the best designed castle in the country in terms of defensive capabilities.

Madog ap Llewelyn, after spending some time on the run, was forced to surrender and taken to the Tower of London where he spent the rest of his life a prisoner. Finally, after twenty years of war, Edward was sole master of Wales.

SOURCE 8

Beaumaris Castle, Edward's final Welsh castle, started in 1295 and costing around £20,000.

FOCUS TASK

Why was Edward able to defeat the Welsh? Part 2

Now that you have made your factor cards, complete the following activities to explain how the English defeated the Welsh:

1 Rank the cards in each pile into importance, with the most important at the top of the pile, and the least important at the bottom.
2 Use your sorted cards to write your own answer to the following question:

'Why was Edward able to defeat the Welsh?'

TOPIC SUMMARY

The invasion and colonisation of Wales

- Edward claimed overlordship of Wales and expected the Welsh leader, Llywelyn ap Gruffudd, to acknowledge this.
- Llywelyn repeatedly refused to do so and this led to a series of wars.
- England's wealth meant Wales found it hard to oppose Edward, and many Welshmen fought on the side of England.
- Edward built a string of castles to make sure Wales stayed peaceful.
- There were Welsh rebellions in 1282–83, 1287 and 1294.
- Edward worked hard, and spent a lot of money he could scarcely afford, in controlling Wales.
- Wales became, in effect, a COLONY of England.

3.3 The Great Cause: Relations with Scotland

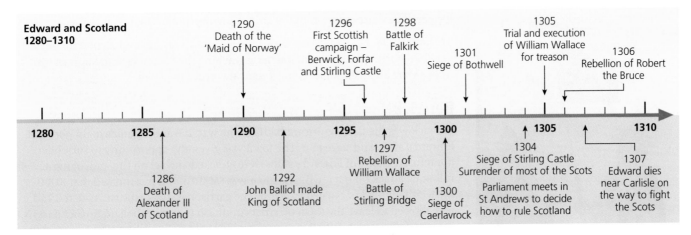

Edward and Scotland 1280–1310

1290 Death of the 'Maid of Norway'

1296 First Scottish campaign – Berwick, Forfar and Stirling Castle

1298 Battle of Falkirk

1301 Siege of Bothwell

1305 Trial and execution of William Wallace for treason

1306 Rebellion of Robert the Bruce

1280 — 1285 — 1290 — 1295 — 1300 — 1305 — 1310

1286 Death of Alexander III of Scotland

1292 John Balliol made King of Scotland

1297 Rebellion of William Wallace

Battle of Stirling Bridge

1300 Siege of Caerlavrock

1304 Siege of Stirling Castle Surrender of most of the Scots

Parliament meets in St Andrews to decide how to rule Scotland

1307 Edward dies near Carlisle on the way to fight the Scots

FOCUS

The death of Alexander IV triggered a succession crisis in Scotland. Edward was asked to arbitrate between rival claimants, but came to believe he had the right to be king. This led to years of war between England and Scotland. In the end, despite his reputation as 'Hammer of the Scots', Edward was not able to gain effective control of Scotland. This topic examines these events and investigates Edward's successes and failures to explain why he was unable to conquer Scotland.

FOCUS TASK

How successful were Edward's Scottish campaigns? Part 1

As you study this topic gather evidence of Edward's successes and failures in his Scottish campaigns. Write each piece of evidence on a separate card. Use different colour cards for success and failure. At the end you will use this evidence to judge how successful you think Edward was and the reasons for his success or failure.

The Scottish succession: Who should be king?

Alexander III, King of Scotland, died in 1286 without a son. His daughter was married to the King of Norway, and their daughter Margaret, known as the Maid of Norway became the heir. But she was only three years old. The Scottish Parliament appointed six GUARDIANS to rule in her place until she arrived in Scotland and reached maturity. She was betrothed (promised in marriage) to Prince Edward of England, which held out the prospect of a future English king (Edward II) one day ruling both England and Scotland.

Unfortunately for Margaret and for Scotland, on her way from Norway to Scotland, Margaret was taken ill and died in the Orkneys in 1290. There was now no clear heir, although plenty of people claimed the throne. Civil war seemed possible between the main rivals and to avoid this the Scots asked Edward I to judge the claimants. When Edward set up a council in Berwick in 1291 to decide who should be king there were fourteen claimants but only two realistic contenders.

- **John Balliol, 1249–1314:** The Balliol family had lands in both England and Scotland. Balliol was a great-great-great-grandson of King David I through his mother and thus had a strong claim to the throne.
- **Robert the Bruce the Fifth, circa 1210–95:** Robert was also descended from David I, although Balliol's claim was the stronger. He also had lands in both England

and Scotland. He had been REGENT during the MINORITY of Alexander III so was an influential Scottish baron.

On the death of the Maid of Norway, Robert, along with his armed men, marched on Perth. It looked as if he was going to claim the throne by force. This was what pushed Edward into agreeing to get involved in deciding who should be king.

Edward picked Balliol. Some argue that he did this because he thought Balliol would be a weak king, and so feel indebted to Edward and therefore would be easy to control. Once Edward decided Balliol should be king, Bruce retired from public life and went to live on his estates and died in 1295. He renounced his claim to the Scottish throne in favour of his son, also called Robert the Bruce (the Sixth).

It might appear that Edward had averted a crisis. However, over the next three years there was a new crisis, which was partly of Edward's own making! Edward insisted Balliol pay homage to him in Newcastle in 1292. Then he demanded that the Scots supply him with money and troops to fight the French. The Scots had had enough and deposed Balliol, replacing him with twelve Guardians in 1295.

As you might expect, given Edward's reputation as a warrior king, his next move was to plan an invasion of Scotland.

The campaign of 1296

The Scots felt threatened by Edward so made an alliance with France. They also made the first moves, attacking northern England and threatening Carlisle. This increased Edward's support in England, allowing him to finance an army.

In March 1296, Edward, along with a force of 1,000 cavalry and 20,000 infantry, marched north into Scotland, intent on teaching the Scots a lesson. Many of his troops were Scottish, some led by Robert the Bruce the Sixth.

Berwick

Berwick was the first significant battle of the war. It was Scotland's main port and Edward's army laid siege to it. The town was given the opportunity to surrender, but refused. Some of Edward's ships were attacked and set on fire, provoking a full-scale attack on the town. The town was SACKED and it is estimated that 7,000 died, either killed or burned to death. The garrison in the castle surrendered and was allowed to leave the town on strict condition that they took no further part in the war. Edward re-fortified the town, and brought in English settlers to restart the economy as Berwick was now to be an English town.

Dunbar

Dunbar was another resounding victory for the English. Dunbar Castle was the home of the Earl of March, who was fighting with the English. His wife, however, invited Scots into the castle and prepared to defy Edward's army. John Balliol and his army were summoned to help her. On 27 April, two forces of cavalry charged each other and the Scots were easily driven from the field, scattering across the countryside. The next day Edward arrived at the castle to accept its surrender. This was, in effect, the end of the fighting.

Stirling Castle

Edward continued north, reaching Stirling. Stirling Castle and bridge are the gateway to the north of Scotland. It is said that the garrison had fled, leaving a caretaker to hand over the keys! John Balliol was captured, stripped of his regalia and sent to the Tower of London. The Stone of Destiny, above which Scottish kings were crowned, was removed from Scone Abbey and taken to Westminster Abbey by Edward as a sign of his victory. The speed and decisiveness of Edward's victory only enhanced his reputation as a fearsome military leader.

English rule

By the autumn of 1296, Edward had left for England, leaving royal officials to run Scotland for him. David Santiuste, in his recent book *The Hammer of the Scots*, states that 'ten years of rising tensions between England and Scotland had culminated in a military conquest that was accomplished with almost embarrassing ease'. The new administration seemed to place huge demands on the Scots:

- taxes and troops to fight the French
- confiscation of the wool crop by the King to pay some of his debts
- the lands of some of those supporting Balliol given to others, both English and Scottish, who had supported Edward
- feeding the English garrisons.

Even Scots who had supported Edward, such as the Earl of March and Robert Bruce, began to feel alienated by the new regime. Edward was treating Scotland like a colony to be run for his own benefit – and there was no new Scottish king, only Edward.

THINK

1 Why do you think Edward chose Balliol?
2 Why do you think Balliol was unable to unite the Scots?

THINK

3 Was it the strength of England or the weakness of Scotland that led to such an easy victory for Edward in 1296?
4 What did Edward's officials in Scotland do in 1296–97 that made peace unlikely?

William Wallace and the first war of Scottish independence

Very little is known of William Wallace before 1297. He first came to prominence when he murdered the (English) sheriff of Lanark and fled to Selkirk Forest. It is said that the sheriff raped his wife, but there is no proof of that. Whatever the reason, Wallace hated the English and carried out a series of attacks on isolated English GARRISONS, earning a reputation as a successful warrior and winning the support of some, but not all, of the Scottish lords. Inspired by Wallace, others rebelled against the English, including the MacDougalls in the north west, the de Morays (sometimes printed as the Murrays) in the north, and Robert the Bruce in Annandale.

The Battle of Stirling Bridge, 1297

These revolts led to the Battle of Stirling Bridge (see page 66) where Wallace and de Moray defeated the English and sent them scampering out of Scotland. Wallace, in recognition of his victory, was made sole Guardian of Scotland.

Edward responds

Edward was in England and distracted by events there, and in France. He had been forced by his barons to re-issue MAGNA CARTA just a month after Stirling Bridge, because many of his barons didn't trust him (see Factfile). Edward was also having trouble persuading Parliament to vote him a tax so he could fight the Scots. However Wallace helped him out by invading northern England, reaching Durham. This united England and Edward was able, in 1298, to raise an army. Before heading into Scotland, Edward went on pilgrimage to the shrine of St John of Bridlington and St Cuthbert of Durham to seek God's blessing on his invasion.

The Battle of Falkirk, 1298

Edward decisively defeated the Scots at Falkirk in July 1298. The English ARCHERS were Edward's decisive advantage. For all his military experience, Falkirk was only Edward's third set-piece battle – the others had been Lewes in 1264 and Evesham in 1265! None of his campaigns in Wales had required this kind of battle – they had been raids and skirmishes.

It was at Falkirk that Wallace first used the tactic of the schiltrom (circles of infantry protected from cavalry by long spears – see page 52). But they were defeated by English cavalry.

Edward was also helped by Scottish division. Some of the Scot's cavalry left the battlefield, having made a secret deal with Edward in return for land in England. Wallace managed to escape and headed north to safety. Edward's army then, to quote contemporary Scottish chroniclers, 'ravished the land of Scotland', in revenge for what the Scots had done in northern England.

The Pope takes sides

Wallace managed to send EMISSARIES to the Pope who wrote to Edward in 1299, demanding he leave Scotland. The Papal Bull (or letter) states quite clearly that, 'from ancient times the Realm of Scotland was not, is not feudally subject to your predecessors, the kings of England, nor to you'. This Papal Bull carried the threat of EXCOMMUNICATION if not obeyed. Nevertheless, Edward carried on sending armies into Scotland but he could not defeat the scattered Scottish forces.

ACTIVITY

William Wallace

Using the information on pages 63–7, and your own research, put together a short profile of the life of William Wallace, using no more than six bullet points.

FACTFILE

Blessing the Magna Carta

- King John had been forced by his barons to issue Magna Carta in 1215, agreeing to uphold the law.
- Henry III had also re-issued Magna Carta in 1267.
- Edward I was forced by Parliament to re-issue Magna Carta in 1297, agreeing: 'that the great charter of liberties and the forest charter which were made by common agreement of all the realm in the time of King Henry, my father, be kept in all their points.'
- He was forced to re-issue it again in 1300, so he obviously had not changed things to the satisfaction of his Parliament.

Edward's problems

Edward was having difficulty with the Scottish rebels, but he was also having difficulty with the English. Parliament, meeting in Lincoln in 1301, refused him a tax, and the clergy refused him one too. Feudal summons to join the army often went unanswered, as people became increasingly resentful of the cost of Edward's war. One knight, Hugo Fitz Heyer, when summoned to fulfil his feudal duty to join the army with bow and arrow, turned up on the battlefield, fired one arrow in the direction of the Scots in 1300 then went home!

The decisive campaign of 1304–05

Edward did not give up. In 1303, Edward led his fourth invasion of Scotland, with an army of at least 9,500 infantry as well as 3,500 cavalry. In a two-pronged attack, from Carlisle in the west and Berwick in the east, Edward made considerable progress.

Up to 200 ships were used to deliver supplies to both armies. Three wooden bridges were constructed in King's Lynn and shipped to Scotland for crossing the Forth. Edward had learned the lesson of Stirling Bridge. Siege engines were used to lay siege to castles, especially Stirling Castle (see page 52).

Most Scots, including John Comeyn, one of the leading barons, submitted to Edward by early February 1304. Edward spent the winter in Dunfermline, ready to continue the campaign in the spring. In March 1304, Edward held a Parliament in St Andrews to sort out arrangements for ruling Scotland. Perhaps learning from his previous mistake in 1296, Edward promised that, 'all laws, customs usages and franchises be kept in all parts as they were in the time of Alexander III'. The Englishman, John of Brittany, was put in charge of the government of Scotland, but of the 22 sheriffs, eighteen were Scots. Some leading Scots were exiled, but most were pardoned and managed to retain their lands.

The death of Wallace

A reward was placed on Wallace's head. In August 1305, Wallace was betrayed and captured and taken to London in chains. He was tried and, like Dafydd ap Gruffudd before him, found guilty of treason and hanged, drawn and quartered. His head was placed on a spike on the Tower of London and the four quarters of his body sent to be displayed in Newcastle, Berwick, Stirling and Perth (see Source 3).

King Robert the Bruce

By 1305, it seemed Edward was undisputed master of Scotland. However, Robert the Bruce was not prepared to go along with the other Scottish barons and live peacefully under Edward. At a meeting with John Comyn (who was a descendent of John Balliol and therefore had a claim of his own to the Scottish throne), he stabbed Comyn to death. Bruce was then crowned King of Scotland, although his actions had driven Scotland into civil war, splitting families and communities. Bruce was outlawed by Edward and excommunicated by the Pope. Nevertheless he continued fighting a guerrilla campaign against the English.

Edward: 'Hammer of the Scots'?

In February 1307, the Scots rebelled against the English, again. Edward, despite being unwell, gathered his army and headed north. By early July he had reached Burgh by Sands, in Cumbria. On the morning of 7 July, when his servants went to wake him, he died in their arms. It is said that his last wish was for his bones to be carried with the army until the Scots were defeated! Others said he wanted his heart to be taken to the Holy Land to help defeat the SARACENS.

THINK

Study Source 3.

1 What crimes is William Wallace accused of?
2 From what you have learned, do you think William Wallace sought to call himself King of Scotland?
3 Why are the English claiming he did?
4 Why are John of Lincoln and Roger of Paris claiming 61 shillings and 10 pence from the people of London?
5 Why do you think Edward was so vindictive towards William Wallace?

SOURCE 4

A near-contemporary image of Robert the Bruce and his wife, Elizabeth de Burgh. Bruce was King of Scotland from 1306 until his death in 1329.

Edward's embalmed body was taken south and left lying in state in Waltham Abbey. He was buried in Westminster Abbey on 27 October 1307, in a plain tomb made of Purbeck marble. A Latin inscription, 'Here is Edward I, HAMMER OF THE SCOTS, 1308. Keep the Vow' can still be seen painted along the side of the tomb. This inscription was probably added in the sixteenth century. 'The vow' refers to his promise to defeat Robert the Bruce.

The vow was not fulfilled. Robert the Bruce continued his struggle against the English and he was able to decisively defeat the English at Bannockburn in 1314 ensuring Scotland's continued independence from England.

Memorials to William Wallace

SOURCE 5

The Wallace Memorial, built in 1869 and funded by public donations. It stands, on Abbey Craig, near the site of the Battle of Stirling Bridge, and on reputedly the spot from where Wallace watched the opening stages of the battle. You can see the river in the background.

SOURCE 6

A memorial erected to William Wallace in London, near the spot of his execution, in 1956.

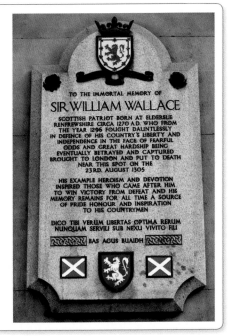

THINK

6 Why might the Scots build this memorial to William Wallace in 1869 (see Source 5?

7 Why might the English build a memorial in London in 1956 (see Source 6)?

8 What are the similarities, and differences, between the memorials?

9 The English memorial is near the site of his execution; the Scottish memorial the site of his greatest victory. What does that tell us about the way Wallace is remembered?

FIGURE 7

A map showing the Battle of Stirling Bridge.

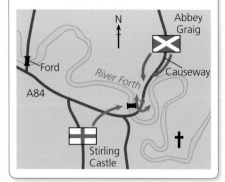

Case Study: The Battle of Stirling Bridge

Location

One of the most significant battles in the war between England and Scotland was the Battle of Stirling Bridge. It was the battle that made William Wallace's reputation. Let's examine this in more detail. By August 1297, William Wallace and Andrew de Moray controlled most of the north of Scotland between them. An English army was sent north to relieve the English garrison marooned in Dundee. Stirling was the first bridge across the Firth of Forth and was thus a strategic point. It was a narrow wooden bridge, scarcely wide enough for two horses to cross side by side.

The Scots were on the north bank of the river, and the English on the south bank. The north end of the bridge led into a marshy area where it would be difficult for an army to deploy effectively. There was a mile-long causeway leading north from the river. A Scottish knight who had joined the English – he hated Wallace more than he hated the English – pointed out that there was a ford a couple of miles upstream that would be much safer to use, where soldiers could safely cross the river ten abreast, but his advice was ignored.

The Battle

Two Dominican friars were sent to Wallace to accept his surrender, but they returned shortly afterwards with William Wallace's first recorded speech: 'Tell your commander that we are not here to make peace but to do battle, defend ourselves and liberate our kingdom.' Wallace was determined to fight, despite being greatly outnumbered. Source 8 tells us what happened next.

SOURCE 8

From *The Chronicle of Walter of Guisborough*, ed. H. Rothwell, Camden Society, 1957. Walter de Guisborough was an English monk who wrote a history of England around 1300. Many of the people involved in Edward's wars with Scotland stopped off at his priory in Yorkshire on the way to and from Scotland, and his priory, one of the richest in the country, was on land given to the Church by Robert the Bruce.

The English army headed towards Stirling Bridge … And the Earl commanded that they should go up to the bridge and cross it. It was astonishing to say, and terrible in its consequence, that such a large number of individual men, though they knew the enemy was at hand, should go up to a narrow bridge which a pair of horsemen could scarcely and with difficulty cross at the same time …

So there crossed over the King's and the Earl's standard-bearers …. and when the enemy had seen that as many had come forth as they could overcome, as they believed, they then came down from the mountain, and sent the spearmen to occupy the foot of the bridge, such that from then no passage or retreat remained open, but in turning back, as also in making haste over the bridge, many were thrown headlong and were drowned …

At length some from amongst those who were left crossed the water by swimming. Also one soldier from our men crossed the water with difficulty on an armed horse.

Aftermath

Over 5,000 English infantry and about one hundred cavalry died in the battle. Scottish casualties are unknown. After the battle, the Earl of Surrey, commander of the English army, panicked and fled south to Berwick, leaving the garrisons in Stirling Castle and Dundee isolated, and surrendering the lowlands of Scotland to the Scottish armies. Such was the hatred of the English officials that it is said by some that the skin of Hugh de Cressingham, Edward's ruler in Scotland who was killed in the battle, was flayed from his body and used by Wallace to make a belt for his sword! William Wallace was made sole Guardian of Scotland as a result of his greatest victory over the English. Stirling Bridge put renewed hope in the Scots, and made life much more difficult for Edward, both in Scotland and in England.

THINK

1   Look carefully at Figure 9 and then read Source 8. To what extent do they agree or disagree with each other?
2   Which is more convincing, the contemporary source or the modern illustration? Why?
3   Why was the location of Stirling Bridge so significant?
4   To what extent was the disaster at Stirling Bridge the fault of the English generals?
5   Why was the result of the Battle of Stirling Bridge so significant?

FIGURE 9

A modern illustration of the Battle of Stirling Bridge. It was drawn in 1976 for a children's story book.

FOCUS TASK

How successful were Edward's Scottish campaigns? Part 2

You have been gathering evidence of Edward's successes and failures in Scotland. Use this evidence to answer these questions.

1 What was Edward's greatest success in Scotland?
2 What was his greatest failure?
3 How close did he come to winning control?
4 How united were the Scots against Edward?
5 What mistakes did Edward make in his campaigns in Scotland?
6 In your opinion, does Edward deserve the epitaph 'Hammer of the Scots'?

Use your notes from Topic 3.2 to compare events in Wales and Scotland.

7 What are the similarities and what are the differences between Edward's campaigns in Wales and Scotland?
8 Why do you think Edward was never called 'Hammer of the Welsh'?

TOPIC SUMMARY

Relations with Scotland

- Edward was asked in to help choose the next king of Scotland but tried to take control himself.
- He chose a puppet ruler, John Balliol, who he thought he could control, and tried to tax the Scots to pay for his wars.
- Dissatisfaction with King John Balliol and opposition to Edward turned into full-scale revolt in 1296, so Edward invaded Scotland quickly crushing Scottish resistance.
- William Wallace emerged as the leader of the Scottish opposition to Edward from 1297 to his death in 1305.
- The Scots were divided. Some supported and fought with Edward, while others supported Wallace. Some, such as Robert the Bruce, changed sides several times.
- In 1306 Robert the Bruce was made King of Scotland and resistance started all over again.
- In 1307 Edward died on the way north to fight Bruce. Bruce continued his guerrilla campaign and eventually defeated the English at the Battle of Bannockburn in 1314, ensuring Scotland's continued independence from England, despite all Edward's efforts.

REVIEW OF CHAPTER 3
Edward I's military campaigns in Wales and Scotland

REVIEW TASK

What kind of king was Edward I?

Look back at the introduction to this book, and especially the answer you wrote to the question, 'What kind of king do you think Edward was?' You are now going to review that answer in the light of the work you have completed in Chapter 3.

Part 1

Here is our list of what people expected of a medieval king:

- to defend the country
- to produce an heir
- to keep the law
- to protect the Church
- to ensure people can go about their daily lives in safety and freedom.

1 Which of these aspects of kingship have been dealt with in Chapter 3?

2 How well do you think Edward has dealt with these aspects of kingship?

Part 2

Draw up a 'living graph', like the one below, and plot each event above or below the line, depending on whether this shows Edward acting in his own self-interest, or in the interests of 'good government' and the people. The higher or lower you place an event, the stronger it fits that description.

It is possible that an action is in both Edward's and the people's interest, for example, in 1297 when Edward re-issued Magna Carta. This was in order to persuade the Commons to vote him a tax and to prevent a civil war. Does this show Edward acting in his own self-interest? Yes, it probably does, and so should appear above the line by quite some way. You could also plot this event below the line, as it can be interpreted as in the peoples' interests too.

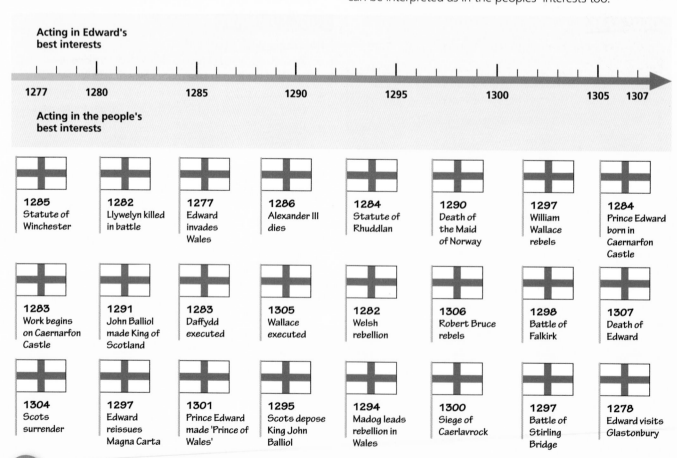

Acting in Edward's best interests

1277   1280   1285   1290   1295   1300   1305   1307

Acting in the people's best interests

1285 Statute of Winchester	**1282** Llywelyn killed in battle	**1277** Edward invades Wales	**1286** Alexander III dies	**1284** Statute of Rhuddlan	**1290** Death of the Maid of Norway	**1297** William Wallace rebels	**1284** Prince Edward born in Caernarfon Castle
1283 Work begins on Caernarfon Castle	**1291** John Balliol made King of Scotland	**1283** Daffydd executed	**1305** Wallace executed	**1282** Welsh rebellion	**1306** Robert Bruce rebels	**1298** Battle of Falkirk	**1307** Death of Edward
1304 Scots surrender	**1297** Edward reissues Magna Carta	**1301** Prince Edward made 'Prince of Wales'	**1295** Scots depose King John Balliol	**1294** Madog leads rebellion in Wales	**1300** Siege of Caerlavrock	**1297** Battle of Stirling Bridge	**1278** Edward visits Glastonbury

Practice questions

Here is another opportunity to use practice questions to review your learning. In your exam you will be set four questions on the British depth study.

Question 1 will be 'an interpretation question'. You should aim to use your knowledge to explain how convincing an interpretation is. The interpretation could be written or visual. For example:

1. How convincing is Interpretation A in helping us understand medieval warfare? (8 marks)

INTERPRETATION A

A modern illustration of English knights attacking a Scottish schiltrom.

For this question you should aim to describe what you can see and then use detailed knowledge to support and contradict what the source tells you about medieval warfare. Try to find at least three points on either side – convincing and not convincing. Use the questions below to help you get started.

- Are the infantry dressed as suggested on page 51?
- Are the cavalry dressed as suggested on page 50?
- Can you identify the weapons used by both infantry and cavalry?
- How secure do the wooden stakes seem?
- Have the cavalry been stopped by the wooden stakes?
- What devices has the artist used to make his picture appear more dramatic?

Question 2 will ask you to 'explain' something, for example, some development or change in the period. It is testing your knowledge and understanding. For example:

2. Explain what was important about Edward's Welsh castles. (8 marks)

There are many things you could cover but you should focus on those that show the importance of the Welsh castles in Edward's conquest of Wales, not the incidental details about particular castles.

1. Which of the following do you think you should spend most time on?
   - secure bases for army and administration
   - visual reminder of Edward's power
   - on the coast (could be supplied by sea) unable to be cut off by the Welsh
   - Caernarvon deliberately designed to remind people of Constantinople and imperial power
   - Edward liked building castles.
2. Look back at Topic 3.2 to see how you could expand on your chosen point.

Question 3 asks you to write an account. This is a 'narrative' question, testing your knowledge and understanding and analysis of historical events. For example:

3. Write an account of the ways warfare changed during the reign of Edward I. (8 mark)

For this question you should aim to cover a range of events and developments in enough detail to show that you understand the different aspects of warfare and what was changing. You could include:

- size and composition of his army
- winter campaigns, as in Wales in 1282
- supplies for the army
- weapons and tactics used in siege warfare
- castle design, as in Beaumaris, in order to consolidate victories.

Look back at Topic 3.1 and write a paragraph on at least one of these points. make sure you connect it back to the focus of the question which is about the changes in warfare.

Question 4 will be on the historic environment. You will be given a statement about the period and you will have to reach a judgement on how far a historical site you have studied supports the statement. You should be balanced and analytical but the key will be to make a judgement about how far the statement is true and to write a coherent essay to back up your judgement.

We don't know which site you will study as it changes every year but you can practice with any site. One of the sites that has been mentioned in this chapter is Caernarvon Castle (see page 31).

Read the information on pages 59–60 about Caernarvon Castle and the Example question 4 on page 23.

What do you think would be a good statement to make about the significance of castles in Edward's campaigns in Wales and Scotland that could be tested through a study of Caernarvon Castle in particular?

SOURCE 1

The Eleanor Cross at Geddington today.

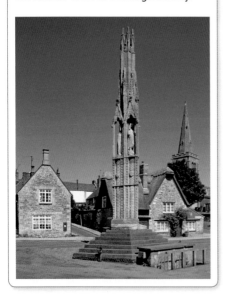

SOURCE 2

One of the statues of Eleanor on the Geddington Cross today.

Conclusion: How should we remember Edward?

There were many different sides to Edward I as king. So how should he be remembered?

Family man?

Edward married Eleanor of Castile in 1254 when they were both very young. It was an arranged marriage, yet they seem to have fallen madly in love. Eleanor gave birth to Joan when on a Crusade with Edward, and gave birth to Edward in the chaos of Caernarvon Castle in 1284. They had fifteen children, although not all survived childhood. (Edward had three more children by his second wife, Margaret.) When Eleanor died in November 1290, Edward was devastated. He wrote, 'Living, I loved her dearly and I shall never cease to love her in death'. She died at Harby, on the borders of Nottinghamshire and Lincolnshire, on a tour of her properties. Edward was at her bedside as she died. The business of government came to a complete standstill for several days following Eleanor's death.

Eleanor's body was embalmed and the viscera (internal organs) were buried in Lincoln Cathedral. Her body, accompanied by Edward and a huge entourage, headed for Westminster Abbey and a state funeral. At each overnight stop (there were twelve of them in total), Edward ordered the building of a memorial cross. Only parts of three crosses remain today, and the best preserved of these is at Geddington (see Source 1) despite having lost its 'immense' cross from the top of the monument.

The story of the Eleanor Crosses is a love story without parallel in the history of England. Edward waited a long nine years before remarrying and his daughter who was born in 1305 was named Eleanor.

The Eleanor Cross at Geddington

- The Eleanor Cross at Geddington was erected, probably in 1294, opposite St Mary Magdalene Church, where the cortège had rested on the night of 6 December 1290, next to a royal hunting lodge. The hunting lodge had hosted Henry II, Henry III, King John and King Richard in the past, and had even been used for a royal summit involving the kings of England and Scotland.
- The cross was built in the new, highly ornamental English Decorated style, using local limestone.
- Intricately carved with floral patterns, the slender cross is triangular in plan and stands nearly 12.8 metres (42 feet) tall.
- It is built in three tiers. Below the tapering pinnacle at the top are three canopied NICHES, each containing a Caen stone figure of Eleanor. Beneath these figures are six shields, two on each face, bearing the arms of Castile, Leon, England, and Ponthieu in France, of which Eleanor was countess.

Subsequent history of the Eleanor Crosses

- Most of the crosses were destroyed by Cromwell and his men during the English Civil War, although some were damaged before that during the Reformation when all signs of 'Popery' were removed from churches.
- Several replicas have been made, both in the nineteenth and twentieth centuries, and the remaining three have been subject to some restoration work.

Fighting man?

We have already seen how Edward loved taking part in tournaments as a young man. He also took part in several pitched battles and a Crusade. Much of his life was spent in conflict with Wales, France and Scotland, and he emerged with a reputation as a brave and fearless fighter, as well as a good general. It was perhaps his role in the Ninth Crusade, preserving Acre from the Saracens, which cemented his reputation as a leader of men, although he was only involved in skirmishes whilst in the Holy Land. He seems to have learned from the failures in battle of his father Henry III and his campaigns in Wales and Scotland mostly involved meticulous attention to detail and careful logistical preparation. He also seems to have learnt from his disastrous part in the Battle of Lewes in 1264, where his cavalry charge destroyed the opposition but lack of discipline and chasing the enemy meant that by the time his men returned to the battlefield, the battle was lost.

But how might the Welsh and the Scots consider Edward's fighting abilities?

Successful king?

Again, you have already considered whether or not you think Edward was a successful medieval king. The big question is, when he died, did Edward leave England in a better position than when he became king? Henry III was obviously a weak king, and Edward set out to restore both justice for all and his own rights. In the first part of his reign, law and order improved, new laws were passed aimed to make life fairer, corrupt officials were dismissed and replaced, and trade prospered. But later in his reign, wars with Wales and Scotland preoccupied him, and criminality increased; hence the need for the Statute of Trailbaston, for example (see page 45).

In the latter part of his reign, disputes with Parliament were frequent, and Edward was forced to reissue Magna Carta in 1297 and 1300, promising to maintain liberties and freedoms granted in 1215. Also, in the latter part of Edward's reign, the economy began to falter – there were poor harvests and the wool trade diminished, leading to poverty and crime. War was expensive, and the King was greatly in debt by the end of his reign.

Perhaps the key question to consider, therefore, is when he died, did Edward leave England stronger or weaker? More secure? More united? Edward was the first medieval king not to be faced with a civil war, although it came close in 1295. Perhaps success in Wales and France, and seemingly in Scotland in 1296, deflected the barons from civil war; or perhaps Edward gave them enough concessions to prevent opposition? You decide!

DEBATE

How should we remember Edward?

- Morris (2008) gives his biography of Edward I the title, *A Great and Terrible King*.
- Santiuste (2015) argues Edward was 'respected throughout Europe as a soldier and a statesman.'
- Rees Davis, a Welsh historian, describes the conquest of Wales by Edward I as a 'national disaster that led to a 'national' revolt under Owain Glyndŵr in 1400.'
- Robert the Bruce once declared about Edward and his son 'I am more afraid of the bones of the father dead, than of the living son; and, by all the saints, it was more difficult to get a half a foot of the land from the old king than a whole kingdom from the son!'

FOCUS TASK

Edward's obituary

You are going to write an obituary for Edward I.

1 In order to help you think about what to include in your obituary, first look online for an obituary of someone you have already studied in history.
2 Makes notes on what is included and what is excluded from the obituary you are studying.
3 Now write your own obituary of Edward, using no more than 500 words. Consider what the main changes were during Edward's reign, and think about what you will include and what you will omit from the obituary.

ASSESSMENT FOCUS

How the British depth studies will be assessed

The British depth studies will be examined in Paper 2. All four British depth studies will be on the same paper so make sure you pick the right one! The questions could be on any part of the content so you should aim to know it all. It will test three of the assessment objectives:

- AO1 – knowledge and understanding
- AO2 – explanation and analysis
- AO4 – interpretations.

Using practice questions for revision

When you are revising, it is sometimes a good idea to attempt a practice question before re-reading the relevant section in the textbook. You don't need to write the answer in full before you re-read the text. You could plan an answer, or draw up a spider diagram or list of ideas before. The important thing is to try very hard to remember *before* you check what you have done. Once you have re-read the relevant section of the textbook, then you should try to write a full answer.

The exam questions

Question 1 will focus on interpretations. You will be given one visual or written interpretation of some aspect of the specification content, for example about a named individual, a battle or a development. You will be asked to comment on how accurately this reflects what you think happened. For example:

> 1. How convincing is this interpretation about Robert Burnell's value to Edward I?
>
>   Explain your answer using Interpretation A and your contextual knowledge. (8 marks)

> ### INTERPRETATION **A**
>
> From The Thirteenth Century by Maurice Powicke, OUP 1962, pp. 336–38.
>
> *Robert Burnell was a great man who enjoyed the special friendship of the king. But though he was very close to the king, he remained his servant. Edward declared that no-one knew him better or could carry out his wishes better than Burnell. He made him feel safe.*

The question is asking you to compare Interpretation A with what you know (your contextual knowledge) about this location and explain how accurately it portrays what you know. Do not focus only on things that are incorrect as it is just as important to look for accuracies and things that it does not tell you. The important thing is to use your knowledge and judge the overall feel of the interpretation and the detail.

In some ways this interpretation is quite convincing as we know that Robert Burnell served Edward before he was king and as Chancellor from 1274 until his death in 1292. We know that Burnell was completely trusted by Edward and acted as an efficient 'gatekeeper' to the King. Throughout the period, writs and warrants were issued by Burnell without reference to Edward. Burnell was even Governor of Gascony for a time!

Most historians maintain that Burnell was accessible, even-handed and principled in applying the aims and ideas of Edward, although he did manage to amass a huge personal fortune as Chancellor, as evidenced by the many estates he bought and the construction of Stokesay Castle.

However, the interpretation does not provide evidence or examples to back up the author's assertions, and that leads us to question its utility. Nevertheless, the fact that Burnell remained Chancellor for nearly twenty years and retained the complete trust of Edward suggests that Edward relied on Burnell, and that Burnell depended on his position to enrich himself and his family.

> - This answer addresses some important points, on both sides of the question, things that make the interpretation convincing and less convincing.
> - The answer suggests a reason the interpretation was produced and its potential use was for the general public, not academics. It uses contextual knowledge to support analysis of the interpretation.

Over to you

Write two more sentences that assess how convincing the interpretation is in dealing with portraying Burnell's value to Edward.

Question 2 will ask you to explain some 'historical event, issue or development'. It might be about:

- The importance of some key feature or characteristic of a period.
- The causes and consequences of the event.
- The nature and degree of change associated with the event – how much changed, whether some things changed more than others, how much remained the same.

For example:

> 2. Explain what was important about Parliament in Edward I's time. (8 marks)

There is more to this than knowledge. You should aim to select the knowledge that is relevant to the question, write in clear language and include plenty of relevant detail to support your answer. The focus of the question is on the role of Parliament, so the points you make and the knowledge that you use to support those points should focus on changes to the role of Parliament throughout Edward's reign.

Parliament under Edward had more power than under previous monarchs. Both its composition and its powers changed during Edward's time. Simon de Montfort is often called the 'Father of Parliament' for inviting the commons in 1265, but Edward's first Parliament in 1275, called to ratify the Statute of Westminster, was the largest medieval Parliament ever. The 'Model Parliament' of 1295 was perhaps the first to function much as a modern parliament does. Parliament's power was shown when, in 1297, Parliament was reluctant to grant a tax to Edward, and forced him to re-issue Magna Carta, and also how Parliament limited Edward's ability to fight the Scots by refusing finance.

Perhaps the greatest change was that Parliament initially was largely supportive of Edward and his attempts to remove corruption and rule fairly, but towards the end of his reign there was much more tension between King and Parliament.

This answer seems like a good one, because it explains changes in both composition and powers of Parliament, and develops this answer by suggesting changes between the start and end of Edward's rule.

However, the composition of Parliament and the real causes of the conflict between Edward and Parliament need exploring in more detail.

Over to you

1 Why was Parliament reluctant to grant taxes to Edward?
2 Was the composition of Parliament always the same when it met under Edward?
3 What events could we use to help make this answer better explain the importance of Parliament?

Question 3 asks you to write a narrative account of some change or development from the period and, within the narrative, explain the development as directed by the question.

For example:

> 3. Write an account of the way the economy changed during Edward's reign. (8 marks)

The big difference between Questions 2 and 3 is that in Question 3 you are required to write an orderly account of what happened and of the way in which the events you describe over time affected Edward's England. So this is still not 'everything you know about' a topic. You should still select knowledge carefully that shows you understand these developments and their effects.

Most people worked in agriculture and lived in the country throughout Edward's reign. Agriculture did well for 30 years up to around 1295, then poor harvests caused difficulties for many. The economy became more cash based, with many peasants growing cash crops to supply the new towns, as well as keeping sheep for their wool. However, some estates, especially those owned by the Church, were more conservatively run and found it hard to change. Of course, if you were a villein you often had no choice, but people could use the new opportunities to get rich. Laurence of Ludlow is a perfect example of this – he was a very successful wool merchant.

England's economy was increasingly integrated into that of Europe, selling wool and importing wine and other luxuries. People might escape to the new and growing towns and find new economic opportunities there, but without a doubt, wool was the key to wealth.

This answer distinguishes between farming and the wool trade. It highlights the growth of a cash economy, and England's closer trading ties to Europe. However, the new crops and means to make money are not explained in much detail, and these opportunities are not the only ones that you could have written about.

- You could have written more about Edward's taxes on the wool trade and the impact these had on the wealth of the country.
- You could also write in more detail about the new trades and opportunities in the towns.

Over to you

Find out more about these changes from the textbook and write another paragraph about the significance of the merchants and overseas trade.

Question 4, which carries the highest marks, is an essay question based on a specific place (an historic environment) such as a castle, a manor house, a monastery or a battle field. For example:

> 4. 'The mainreason for Edward I's success in conquering Wales was the building of castles.' How far does a study of Beaumaris Castle support this statement?
>
>   Explain your answer. You should refer to Beaumaris Castle and your contextual knowledge. (16 marks)

Your aim is to use your knowledge of the period to connect this site – in this case Beaumaris Castle – and its features and its significance to the wider developments you have studied in the rest of the depth study. You will be told what the site will be in advance of the exam and you will have studied it. However, you will not be told the specific aspect of it that the question will focus on. You will be given a statement about the period which connects to the site and you will need to write an extended essay using your knowledge about the site and about the period to show how this statement is true.

You need to know your site well to write an essay but, equally importantly, you also need to think clearly in order to develop a clear, coherent and relevant argument from the start, and carry it through the whole essay supporting your argument.

King Edward dealt very effectively with rebellion in Wales, and his new castles played a strong role in this.

Edward built the castles, both to intimidate the Welsh and prevent further rebellion. Most of the Welsh castles were similar in design, for example the wharf so it could be supplied by sea, and the concentric style, but as an example of English power Beaumaris was special and different in some ways from the other castles. For instance it has been described as the 'perfect' concentric castle. As it was one of the last to be built (but never finished) it incorporated all the latest defensive technology. It was designed to dominate Anglesey, and ensure there were no more Welsh rebellions. Also, unlike Edward's other castles it was started after the final Welsh rebellion of 1294, probably as a pointed response to that rebellion, although plans for the castle date from around 1284.

However, building these castles did not stop rebellion by the Welsh. The incomplete Caernarvon Castle and new town were burnt down in the Welsh rebellion of 1294, but immediately Edward began to rebuild them. There were rebellions in 1282–83, 1287 and 1294. Edward spent thousands of pounds in defeating the Welsh, and even when he was really short of money towards the end of his reign he continued to build Beaumaris Castle. When work stopped, around 1330, £15,000 had been spent on the still-incomplete castle.

The most important changes brought about by these castles and their accompanying new towns were both the settlers they brought in their wake, and also the very size of the castles which did finally cower the Welsh rebels into submission. The fact that there were no more rebellions against Edward after 1294 might suggest that Beaumaris was successful in Edward's aim to build castles to remove the threat of rebellion.

Edward's castles did not, by themselves, smash the Welsh and end rebellion. They were an integral part of Edward's strategy to defeat the Welsh rebels and in effect turn Wales into another part of England.

Over to you

The most successful answers will focus on particular aspects of the site. Read through these and see if you can identify where in this answer these things are covered. Which bits are missing and could be added?

- location, structure, and design
- the way the site was used
- people connected with the site
- how the site reflects culture, values and fashions of Edward's England
- how the site links to important events and/or developments during Edward's rule.

Keys to success

As long as you know the content and have learned how to think, this exam should not be too scary. The keys to success are:

1 **Read the question carefully**. Identify the skill focus (what they are asking you to do) the content focus (what it is about) and select from your knowledge accordingly.
2 **Note the marks available**. That helps you work out how much time to spend on answering each question.
3 **Plan your answer before you start writing**. The golden rule is: know what you are going to say, then say it clearly and logically.
4 **Check your work**. Try to leave some time at the end to check for obvious spelling mistakes, missing words or other writing errors that might cost you marks.

This short introduction clearly signposts the different sections of this answer, and gives the reader an idea of the writer's final conclusion.

This part of the answer is about the similarities and differences between Beaumaris and other Welsh castles built by Edward. One thing that is missing is detail about the immediate impact of building these castles. Use pages 56–7 to find out some of the immediate impact and make a brief list of things that you could add to this section.

The first sentence of this paragraph signposts to the reader that we've moved on to thinking about ways in which the castles did not stop Welsh rebellions, but still relates this to Beaumaris Castle. What it does not consider is the part harsh English rule played in causing rebellion.

Can you spot the phrase that is used to tell the reader about the relative importance of these changes?

This section is the conclusion, and it directly answers the question by reaching a judgement which is clearly supported by the rest of the answer. This isn't the only way of writing this answer. We might also have written about how the castles were an over-reaction to a relatively small Welsh threat, after all, many Welsh fought on the side of Edward. And you might even disagree and argue instead that the castles did not stop rebellion. Don't forget to mention that Beaumaris Castle was never finished, and many of the buildings planned were never completed!

GLOSSARY

ALIENS   Someone from a different country

APPRENTICE   Someone signed up for seven or ten years to work with a craftsman to learn a trade

ARBITRATION   Where both parties in a dispute try, through a person without an interest in that dispute, to reach an agreement.

ARCHAEOLOGISTS   People who study human history through the excavation of historical sites

ARRANGED MARRIAGE   Marriage organised by parents, not by the couple involved

BURGESSES   Freemen in a town, usually the wealthier citizens

CANON   Member of the Church, but not a priest; does some of the jobs priests do

CASH ECONOMY   An economy in which financial transactions are made by cash

CASTLES   A large building, fortified against attack with thick walls, battlements, towers, and often a moat

CELIBATE   Not allowed to marry or have sex

CHANCELLERY   Office of the Lord Chancellor, the King's chief officer

CHIVALRY   Set of rules for knights

CINQUE PORTS   Ports in Kent and East Sussex which traditionally supplied the King with ships in times of war

COIN-CLIPPING   Cutting silver off part of a coin to use that silver for something else

COLONY   One country owned and run by another

CONVALESCENCE   Period of recovery after illness, getting better

CORRUPTION   Breaking the law, dishonest behaviour, either in terms of power or money

CURTAIN WALLS   Walls surrounding a castle or manor house

CUSTOMS DUTY   Tax charged when you either bring goods into a country (imports) or take goods out of a country (exports)

DECORATED STYLE   Style of church architecture used at the end of the 13th century

DEFAULTED   Failed to pay

DOOM PAINTINGS   Paintings on the inside walls of medieval churches showing what happens to you if you die – either going to Heaven, Hell or Purgatory

DORMITORY   Sleeping area

EMISSARY   Special messenger

ENCLOSED   A field surrounded by hedges, walls or ditches

ESTATE   An amount of land or property

EXCOMMUNICATION   To expel someone out of the Church, stop them going to mass or taking the sacraments

EXPEL   To drive or force out

FAIR   Special market, often held once a year

FELON   Criminal

FEUDAL SYSTEM   Medieval way of organising society, with the King owning all the land and having all the power, and the villeins or peasants at the bottom having none

FREEMAN   Not owned by the Lord of the Manor, owns his own land, can come and go as he pleases

GLEBE LAND   Land in a village used to support the parish priest, owned by the Church

GRIEVANCES   Cause for complaint

GUARDIANS   People chosen to run Scotland while there was no King

GUERRILLA WAR   Where small groups of combatants use tactics such as ambushes, sabotage, raids, hit-and-run tactics, and avoid big battles

GUILDS   Organisations of craftsmen, like trade unions, who work together to protect their own interests

HAMMER OF THE SCOTS   Name given to Edward I after he defeated the Scottish armies

HELM   Helmet

HERMIT   Religious person who lives and prays alone, in a special place, away from other monks, priests, etc.

HOLY LAND   Place where Jesus was born, in the Middle East, around Jerusalem and Bethlehem

HOMAGE   Formal acknowledgement to your lord, he is your superior, you owe his a service

HOMICIDE   Murder

INVESTITURE   Being given an honour or rank, in this case being made the Prince of Wales

JEWS   Group of people descended from the ancient Hebrew tribes of Israel. It was the Jews who persuaded Pontius Pilate to kill Jesus, so they were often, especially in Medieval times, hated by Christians

JUSTICE   Either: fairness in the way people are dealt with, or: a judge

LAW AND ORDER   Preventing crime, respect for the rules, where most people stick to the laws

LAY MEMBERS   Not to do with the Church, otherwise known as temporal

LEGACY   Something left behind after an event, or when someone dies

LIVING   Being made the priest of a parish

LOGIC   Careful reasoning, structuring a valid argument

LOW COUNTRIES   Old name for the Netherlands and Belgium, so called because much of the land is below sea level

MACE   Weapon with a heavy head on a solid shaft used to bludgeon opponents, popular with some knights in medieval times

MADDER   Plant grown to make red dye from its roots

MINORITY   Less than half, or underage

MINTED   The process of making coins

MODEL PARLIAMENT Name given to Edward I's parliament of 1295, because it was the first to include not only members of the clergy (priests and other church officials) and the aristocracy, but also elected members to represent ordinary people

MONEYER Coin maker

NAVE Main space in a church, where the ordinary people stood

NICHE Small space or alcove

NOXIOUS Smelly, polluting, dangerous

OBLIGATIONS A duty to do something which is morally or legally binding

OVERLORD Someone who has power over you, who you acknowledge as your superior

PALISADE Wooden fence around a town or settlement

PERPETUITY For ever

PERSONAL CONFESSOR Your own priest to confess your sins to and ask forgiveness from

PILGRIMAGE To visit a very holy place either to ask forgiveness for sin, or for a cure for an illness

POLYGONAL TOWERS Many-sided, usually eight-sided, towers in a castle or city wall

PRAGMATIC Doing what works best in any situation

PUBLIC SUBSCRIPTION Money donated by the public for a specific purpose

PURGATORY Between Heaven and Hell where your soul might spend time until you are pure enough to go to Heaven

PURVEYANCE The right of the King to take goods when necessary to support himself or his army

RATIFIED Consent to something to make it official

REDEMPTION Being saved from sin or from evil

REFECTORY Place where monks ate

REGENT Ruling in place of a king, usually when the king is too young to rule on their own

RETINUE Followers

RHETORIC The art of persuasive speaking (or writing); language designed to persuade or influence people

RIGHTS A moral or legal entitlement to have or do something

ROYAL PREROGATIVE The King's ability to rule and make decisions on his own, without reference to Parliament or anyone else

SACKED Burnt down and destroyed

SANCTUARY A safe place where you cannot be arrested

SARACENS Name used for Muslims or Arabs in the Middle East by Crusaders

SARCOPHAGUS Coffin

SCOTLAND Country to the north of England

SIEGE ENGINE Device designed to destroy city or castle walls

SILVER BULLION Silver waiting to be made into coins or precious items

SPIRITUAL To do with religion or the Church

STATUTE Law passed by parliament

SUBSISTENCE ECONOMY Growing your own food, making the most of the things you use

TAX A compulsory contribution to the government, charged by the government on income and trade, to pay for running the country

TEMPORAL Not to do with the Church

TITHING A group of ten people, who were responsible for each other's law-keeping

TOURNEY Tournament, mock battle, joust

TRADE Buying and selling goods

TREASURER Responsible for Royal finances

VASSALS People who have an obligation or duty to a feudal lord

VILLEIN Peasant who must work for his Lord of the Manor and cannot leave the manor without permission

WALES Country to the west of England, although there was no rigid boundary between the two

WARDSHIP To come

WARFARE Fighting

WRECKS Ships that are destroyed on or near the coast

INDEX